RC JAMES DIO:
THE MAN ON THE SILVER MOUNTAIN

MEMORIES OF A ROCK 'N' ROLL ICON

By Ian Carroll Author

© 2016

Thanks

Dedicated once again to my ever loving & extremely understanding, wife the lovely **Raine** and my three sons, **Nathan**, **Joshua** & **Rex**

Also thanks to my other supporters including **Laura McCartney** and **Gary Martin** for listening to me going on about how the book was progressing. Also, thanks to the Herald newspaper in Plymouth for their continued support.

Thanks to **Mike Horton**, **Mark Jewitt** and **Karl Woodcock** – for their exceptional driving abilities over the years, the length and breadth of the country and abroad as well.

Also, many thanks to **Daryl Banks**, from Jay, Oklahoma, for giving me faith in producing this product.

Thank you also for all your support and help friends on Facebook and Twitter

This Book is licenced for your personal enjoyment only. If you would like to give this book to another person, please purchase an additional copy for each recipient.
Thank you for supporting the hard work of this author

INTRODUCTION

When I was growing up, Heavy Metal/rock music was my music of choice, it was my life. Back in those days in the late 70's and into the early 80's, we would spend our time listening to the best albums of the moment on a massive 'ghetto blaster, either sitting in the park or at any of the local railway stations, train spotting! Our albums of choice at the time were Saxon 'Wheels of Steel', Judas Priest 'British Steel' and Black Sabbath 'Heaven and Hell'. We went through many batteries back in those days, cranking the music up loud and annoying any passers by.

My favourite of all our choices at the time was the Black Sabbath album and it is still one of my favourite albums to this day. How Ronnie James Dio could pack that 'massive' voice into such a small and tiny frame seemed impossible. Once I knew of his work with Black Sabbath I went to search out his back catalogue of work with Rainbow and was just amazed at the lyrics and the quality of his voice, he was and always will be the quintessential rock and metal frontman and with his passing there was a massive void left in the world of rock music.

I was lucky enough to see him just the once with Black Sabbath, five separate times with Dio and twice with Heaven and Hell, at venues such as Cornwall Coliseum, Hammersmith Odeon, Exeter University Main Hall, Plymouth Pavilions, Monsters of Rock Festival and Sonisphere Festival, all 'classic' performances and all terrifically entertaining shows.

When heavily involved in the midst of writing the book 'From Donington to Download' - which covers the history of the Monsters of Rock and Download festivals at Donington Park in the UK – I was very lucky to have a conversation with the man himself on the phone in my kitchen! All the way from the sunny rock 'n' roll world of the USA to my kitchen in dull, rainy and cloudy Devon, England. We talked for quite a while about his performances at the festival and other work with Heaven and Hell. The following are the two excerpts about when he played with Dio at the festival in '83 and again in '87:

"I remember it being a spectacular event and something we were really proud to take part in, especially since it just after the release of our first album so it was a very special time to present it to an audience, especially a British audience, which was very cool.

Having known the guys from Whitesnake for a long time it was nice to see them again of course and it was the first place that I met the guy who would become our drummer for ten years and that was Simon Wright.

It was the first time that I met Simon and he had just gotten the gig with AC/DC, he was only 18 years old at the time and I knew his wife, she came over and introduced me to Simon and I loved him from the off, what a great kid, just the best. Here was a guy who had played with some other bands, but had never really played with anything of that scale and suddenly he was thrust into the fore of one of the biggest bands on the face of the earth. He handled it so well, he was in awe of them, and he was just a regular person, so that was one of the things that I remember the most of Donington.

It was one of our first gigs; I think that we had played a couple of shows before then, I think we had done some small American tour of some kind and then came over to Britain, so it was our first time in Europe for us.

There was some mud thrown on the first show and it hit a lot of people, but they didn't throw any mud at us and being that we were second on the bill we should have been a good target; those people certainly respected what I had done before with Sabbath and Rainbow, so they gave me the same kind of respect that I always give them."

Monsters of Rock, Donington 1983

"I remember that Jon (Bon Jovi) came over and said that we were all going to go up on stage and sing during their show as a finale. Paul Stanley was there and some people from other bands, so I said that I'd think about it, but I didn't do it, it just wasn't me. I certainly hope that Jon doesn't hold that against me for all those years, but it was my decision and I didn't do it.

The Donington festivals were always handled so well, Maurice Jones who did all those was a really good friend, so it was nice be around people that I had known and liked for a long time.

I just remember the show being somewhat like the show that we did in 1983. It's a spectacular audience that are really into everything and they've always been extremely nice to me, as a matter of fact.

I found that both were great days, but the first one was the best, because it was the first; it was a great time and I remember them both very positively.
I'd love to play it again, with either band, Dio or Heaven And Hell."

Monsters of Rock, Donington 1987

Coming off the phone I was on a high. I had spoken to one of my all time musical heroes and it was even more exciting as I was on the guest list for a Dio show at the Bristol O2 Academy in a few weeks time after the phone call.

I would be travelling to the gig and meeting up with Ronnie for another chat in person, either before or after the gig. But then tragedy struck.

On 29th November, Ronnie's wife Wendy announced to the world that he had been diagnosed as having stomach cancer and was being treated at a specialist cancer treatment centre in Houston, Texas; the world of rock was in total shock and dismay.

To make matters worse, she announced six months later, three days before my birthday, on 16th May 2010 that Ronnie James Dio, the legendary frontman, the personification of pure rock 'n' roll, the main focus of so many iconic rock bands had died; this came only two months after my father had died from cancer and 18 months before my wife, at the time, would also pass away from cancer as well.

The music world was in shock. His funeral took place at the Forest Lawn Funeral Home in Hollywood Hills and many musicians, friends and family members were in attendance.

Fast forward two years and I visited the legends tomb at the cemetery in the Hollywood Hills and it was amazing to see the urns either side of his tomb with the hands doing 'devils horns' on them; a more peaceful place you could never find.

When Lemmy died I wrote the book 'Lemmy: Memories of a Rock 'N' Roll Legend', with money from the sales of the book going to Cancer Research, with this book I aim again to make a considerable donation to cancer research.

So, here we are at the beginning of another book, a book of memories of another, sadly passed, rock 'n' roll icon, with stories from all around the world and some very heartfelt and moving tributes to the great man that was the ultimate frontman, Ronnie James Dio.

Ronnie James Dio
10-07-42 to 16-05-10

RONNIE JAMES DIO MAIN ALBUM DISCOGRAPHY

ELF – Elf (1972)
    Carolina County Ball (1974)
    Trying to Burn the Sun (1975)

RAINBOW – Ritchie Blackmore's Rainbow (1975)
    Rising (1976)
    Long Live Rock 'n' Roll (1978)

BLACK SABBATH – Heaven and Hell (1980)
    Mob Rules (1981)
    Dehumanizer (1992)

DIO – Holy Diver (1983)
    The Last in Line (1984)
    Sacred Heart (1985)
    Intermission –Live – (1986)
    Dream Evil (1987)
    Lock Up the Wolves (1990)
    Strange Highways (1993)
    Angry Machines (1996)
    Inferno: Last in Live (1998)
    Magica (2000)
    Killing the Dragon (2002)
    Master of the Moon (2004)
    Evil or Divine: Live in New York City (2005)
    Holy Diver: Live (2006)
    Dio at Donington UK: Live 1983 &1987 (2010)
    Finding the Sacred Heart: Live in Philly 1986 (2013)
    Live in London, Hammersmith Apollo 1983 (2014)

HEAVEN AND HELL – The Devil You Know (2009)

ARGENTINA

Capital City: Buenos Aires
Population: 43,417,000
Currency: Peso
Bands: Los Abuelos de la Nada, Asinesia

"Dio has not only managed to cross the barriers of language and distance. He has managed to make me, a man from Argentina, experience a whole bundle of feelings and lived moments. I could never get to see him live and that is something that saddens me extremely. However, every time I hear his voice timbre characteristic, I cannot help feeling inspired and wander in a sea of strange feelings that only he is able to achieve in me.

Ronnie James Dio was not only an artist but more. His goodness is recognized and remembered by the whole world; as well as his intense desire to never leave a style that he has characterized throughout his career. That tells of a man with definite values and a great example to follow in terms of hopes and dreams. Surely that is my inspiration to continue in front of my projects and never give up.

As a great fan of his; I swear that this world will never forget him while I live and I will tell the new and future generations about who this wonderful artist and human being was."
Cristian N. Martin (Lanús, Argentina)

"I love Dio a lot.
I love everything about him
Not only that, Dio is the best singer who has existed on Earth, nobody will compare to him...
Dio is THE VOICE...
Here in Argentina there are a lot of people who love him and respect him.
Dio is METAL GOD."
Flavia Angeles Dio (Buenos Aires, Argentina)

BELGIUM

Capital City: Brussels
Population: 11,190,845
Currency: Euro
Bands: Aborted, Ostrogoth, Enthroned

> *Rip Ronnie and much blessings and now horns up."*
> **Patrick Booten (Genk, Belgium)**

"Truly will miss you Dio.
I have seen 4 of you're performances and you're voice was always in great shape. I remember that you had a cold and you sang like the stars with the rainbows together.
How did you do that?????????
Ronnie you didn't even need a warm up before you went on stage, only a pint of beer and half of a joint to calm you're stage fright. You belong to the great ones like Sinatra, Lanza (you're favorite singer) and of course Pavarotti.
What did they have in common????
Besides hard rock/metal? They were blessed with a voice sent from god, and you are the greatest because you were the god of hard rock metal singers.
I hope you catch the rainbow up there and make it shine for you and us. Thank god I can listen to you each day.
Dreams are made to come true ... like Ronnie sings whenever you dream, you holding the key; it opens the door to let you be free
And find the sacred heart. And that's your quest.
Rip Ronnie and much blessings and now horns up."
Patrick Booten (Genk, Belgium)

BRAZIL

Capital City: Brasilia
Population: 205,338,000
Currency: Real
Bands: Sepultura, Shaaman Violator, Angra

"Heaven and Hell performed in São Paulo on 15th and May 16th, 2009.
We did a tour, me and some friends traveled almost 600 km. Anxiety began when it was announced the spectacle in Brazil.
Soon we bought tickets and waited for the day to hit the road. We left on the 15th, Friday 23:30, it was cold but it was a quiet trip. We arrived in the morning and wait all day to enter the Credicard Hall. We went into a bar, and DVD Heaven and Hell and there I thought, we are watching these guys on TV and they are there on our side somewhere, soon we will be face to face with them. It was something crazy to think they were there close.
We entered the show house and an atmosphere full of anxiety, expectation of all for the beginning of the show. Finally appeared on stage, and caused a great emotion, it was amazing to see Ronnie go through my front several times, it was one of the best shows I witnessed. Friendly and attentive Ronnie with the audience singing beautiful for everyone. It was exciting, unforgettable.
Exactly one year after the presentation, I was in São Paulo again. I have been watching the Napalm Death. After the show happened Virada Cultural City of São Paulo, thousands of people in the streets. During the presentation of the Brazilian band Krisiun, there was a break, and then the lead singer Alex Camargo announced Ronnie's death.
From here I have no more words ... are some photos and videos of this historic day for me."
Max Souza (Apucarena, Brazil)

Heaven and Hell

'Bible Black' Tour
Credicard Hall, São Paulo, Brazil
16th May 2009

The Mob Rules
Children of the Sea
I
Bible Black
Time Machine
Fear
Falling Off the Edge of the World
Follow the Tears
Die Young
Heaven and Hell
Country Girl
Neon Knights

BULGARIA

Capital City: Sofia
Population: 7,364,570
Currency: Lev
Bands: Demenzia, Odd Crew, Balkandji

"The monument of Dio in Kavarna (the most unique in the world), from openning of the monument with Dio's Disciples and other rock stars, who visited Kavarna - Jorn Lande, UFO, Primal Fear, BG musicians. There are some photos with the major of Kavarna, me, my friends and fans of Dio."
Plamen Penchev (Kavarna, Bulgaria)

"To the music and the magic voice of Ronnie James DIO - introduced to me by my closest and best friend, who introduced me to Motörhead and the great voice of Lemmy! That was many years ago, when I was 13 years old! Unfortunately my friend died of cancer-3 years ago! So my memories of them - Lemmy and DIO - are closely related with her!
And besides that, I like and love their creativity and voices! They both had some of the most impressive and specific voices in rock music! And their bands were my best friends favourite bands with Black Sabbath and two more bands!
I went to only one concert of Ronnie James Dio, which was in 2005 in town of Kavarna -Bulgaria and I will remember it forever! It was a great concert and I was with my friend! In this town they built a monument to DIO in his honour and memory!
I have a special sentiment to Ronnie James DIO and Lemmy!
In principle I always support similar causes as you do! And that and the fact, that my friend died of cancer, are the reasons that I admire your support of such a noble cause, with your books! Thank you-again! I wish you a great success with all of your books!"
Ekatepna Ctoeba (Sofia Bulgaria)

Dio

**'Master of the Moon' Tour
Kaliakra Stadium,
Kavarna, Bulgaria
7th July 2005**

Killing the Dragon
Egypt (The Chains Are On)
Stargazer
Stand Up and Shout
Holy Diver
Sunset Superman
Don't Talk to Strangers
Man on the Silver Mountain
Long Live Rock 'n' Roll
Shivers
Gates of Babylon
Heaven and Hell
Rainbow in the Dark
The Last in Line
We Rock
The Mob Rules

"Great, big legend!!"
Dobromir Petkov (Sofia, Bulgaria)

Canada

Capital City: Ottawa
Population: 35,985,751
Currency: Canadian Dollar
Bands: Anvil, Rush, Billy Talent, Alexisonfire

"R.I.P. Ronnie"
Dean Baldock (Canada)

GERMANY

Capital City: Berlin
Population: 81,459,000
Currency: Euro
Bands: Rammstein, Scorpions, Accept, Helloween

"I never met Dio personally. But I see the 'Holy Diver' show in Munich. Was brilliant!"
Mark Freier (Munich)

Dio

'Holy Diver' Tour
Alabamahalle, Munich
26th November 1983

Stand Up and Shout
Straight Through the Heart
Shame on the Night
Children of the Sea
Holy Diver
Stargazer
Heaven and Hell
Rainbow in the Dark
Man on the Silver Mountain
Starstruck
Evil Eyes
Don't Talk to Strangers

"R.I.P. R.J.D!!!"
Jan Nosko (Germany)

"A long time ago, I was so proud that Ronnie made a picture together with my new tattoo…"
Matthias Bayer (Konz)

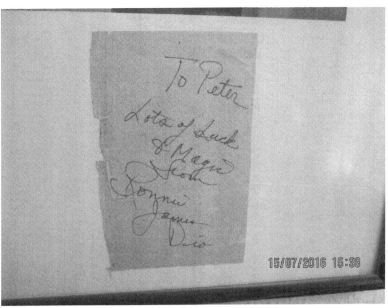

"This Autograph was given at Frankfurt Airport, shortly after the split with Rainbow. I think it was in the early Eighty's. He arrived to make some concerts with Black Sabbath."
Peter Trautner (Frankfurt, Germany)

"For the first time I heard about Dio it was magic.
His voice on the album 'Long Live Rock 'n' Roll' from Rainbow released 1978, blew me away. Since this day I was a big Rainbow fan also.
Then Dio released his first solo record and I heard it on the radio. What a debut. For me the best album by him ever.
In 1984 I saw him for the first time alive on stage. The big open air concerts in Karlsruhe and Nürnberg and the tour with Queensrÿche in Essen the same year. In Essen he touches my heart.
In those days it was allowed to bring professional photo stuff to the concerts. I raise my camera with my tele lens maybe from about the 20th line. He sang the part of 'Rainbow In the Dark' - 'you're just a picture - just an image caught in time we're a lie - you and I' and looked at me and show his fingers to me...what a picture...this moment is in my heart every time I'm listening to this song.
Over the years I saw him twice. I worked for an international magazine so it was a great pleasure for me to meet him personally during 'Popkomm 1996' in Cologne Germany for a press schedule. Also I take some press pictures during this tour in Bonn.
One of the biggest moments was the tour with Sabbath as Heaven and Hell. This was really awesome.
A man a voice that was Dio to me. Great music, fantastic musicians and always a star near by the fans. Gone but never forgotten.
Siegfried Hahn (Herne, Germany)

Dio

'The Last In Line'
Monsters of Rock
Wildparkstadion, Karlsruhe
1st September 1984

Stand Up and Shout
One Night in the City
Mystery
Egypt (The Chains Are On)
Holy Diver
Heaven and Hell
The Last in Line
Rainbow in the Dark
Man on a Silver Mountain
Long Live Rock 'n' Roll
The Mob Rules

GREECE

Capital City: Athens
Population: 10,955,000
Currency: Euro
Bands: Firewind, Nightfall, Septic Flesh,

*"R.I.P. to the God of Heaven and Hell!!!
I live in Athens Greece, and I saw the Divine Short 3 times and 2 with Heaven and Hell. Respect!!!"*
Johnelena Sabbath (Athens, Greece)

Heaven and Hell

'Heaven and Hell' Tour
Terra Vibe, Malakása, Greece
July 1st 2007

The Mob Rules
Children of the Sea
I
The Sign of the Southern Cross
Voodoo
Computer God
Falling Off the Edge of the World
Shadow of the Wind
Die Young
Heaven and Hell
Neon Knights

INDONESIA

Capital City: Jakarta
Population: 255,461,700
Currency: Indonesian Rupiah
Bands: Koil, Kekal, Slank, Superman Is Dead

"Long live DIO."
Carment Roemano (Jakarta, Indonesia)

Capital City: Dublin
Population: 4,635,400
Currency: Euro
Bands: Thin Lizzy, The Answer, Primordial

*"I went to Athens for a karate tournament in 2009 I think it was and it so happened that Heaven and Hell were playing the same time as we were there.
I got a ticket for the gig and I swear to god he was the best vocalist I ever saw and I've seen all the great ones.
I said to one of my friends when I came home that if you closed your eyes you could be listening to a CD.
I will never forget it."*
Garrett O'Donovan (Ireland)

MEXICO

Capital City: Mexico City
Population: 119,530,753
Currency: Peso
Bands: Santana, Rodrigo Y Gabriella, The Chasm

"I'm from Guadalajara, México. I'm not sure if I understand at all, but I have a funny history to tell.
About 1986 I went to preparatory school (3 years before University) in an extreme catholic school, I used to wear my favourite rock n' roll t-shirts. When school authorities watch me wearing my "Last in Line" one, they took me to the principals office, I felt like be a criminal, for them I was a dangerous one. My punishment was to pray the "credo" or leave the school, so I decide to pray.
The fun was that the assistant mic was open to the all campus speakers and everybody heard me pray. When I back to the campus I go ashamed, but People know me as a Dio's fan. 30 years later, there is some guys who remember me for my punishment and I like that!
Long live rock n' roll!
Saludos desde México. Te deseo gran éxito en éste genial proyecto."
Alex Urbina (Guadalajara, Mexico)

"God bless Ronnie..."
Hope Tapia (Mexico)

"The first time I listened to Ronnie, the first time I listened to heavy metal, it changed my life.
I was 12 years old, and had a lot of trouble making friends and getting along. But one day, while playing GTA, I heard 'Holy Diver' in the radio, it had such power and I never went back. I can only thank him and the metal family for making me a better, happier person."
Ilse Eljborn (Mexico)

NETHERLANDS

Capital City: Amsterdam
Population: 16,971,452
Currency: Euro
Bands: Within Temptation, Cirith Gorgor, Altar

"Ronnie James Dio.....
'Butterfly Ball' .. that's the first song I heard of Dio. I immediately fell for this voice...
Later on as I was a bit older about 14, I rediscovered this heavenly evil voice on 'Monsters of Rock' on Sky channel. WE ROCK!!! Goosebumps!! There it was the voice of rock!
Next day I went to the record shop and bought the 'Intermission' live LP, man that was great. I loved his music ever since.
Later I found out about the Black Sabbath era and Rainbow! All the albums are in my collection today, the things this voice does to me, makes me dream, fight and feel alive.
In the year 2000 I was very much into Metalica, Motörhead and Dio and it happened to be Metallica were touring with Dio and they came to Holland playing Groenoord Hallen in Leiden.
I remember my cousin throwing a Snickers bar to the singer of Warrior Soul who were supporting this tour. I asked my cousin: "WHY?"
He replied "I want Dio!"
What more could I say? and hell yeah Dio came, saw and conquered the audience!! 'Rock 'n' Roll Children', 'Last in Line', HEAVEN AND HELL!! and many more.
We sung along as if there was no tomorrow.......Dio........ as I write tears are coming. How I adore his voice, how cool was this original band line up?
Pondering the past, I am so glad I was an 80's metalhead kid.
The best Dio tribute still today is by M.O.D. the Ballad of Dio
Horns up for Dio!
Long live Rock 'N' Roll you man on the Silver Mountain.
Dio and Lemmy made the soundtracks to my youth and I guess my whole life so far.
Töm Justin Case Puch (Ijmond, Netherlands)

Dio

'Lock Up the Wolves' Tour
Groenoordhallen, Leiden
20th May 1990

Wild One
Children of the Sea
Man on the Silver Mountain
Tarot Woman
Stargazer
Long Live Rock 'n' Roll
Born on the Sun
Stand Up and Shout
Why Are They Watching Me
Don't Talk to Strangers
The Last in Line
Heaven and Hell
Rainbow in the Dark

"Still I'm sad."
Erik Engert (Hell, Gelderland, Netherlands)

"From my childhood days in the 1980s I remember the double LP 'Made in Japan' from Deep Purple, my brother had bought it second handed. In particular I remember the track 'Strange Kind of Woman', and making air guitar moves on it together with my brother. Some years later at age 17, I discovered more Deep Purple songs, thanks to the compilation titled 'The Compact Disc Anthology'. I got those two CD's on cassette tapes (used for home purposes only!) and played them over and over. I became a fan and read a lot of things about the band in encyclopedia and magazines, for instance what the band members had done besides Deep Purple.

When I bought my first CD player (1994) and began looking for CD's, I found a second handed copy of Rainbow 'On Stage'. I already knew the Rainbow hit 'Since You've Been Gone' from the radio and kind of liked the 80s A.O.R. sound it had. I also was aware Rainbow had a different singer before that. A singer I already knew from the Roger Glover song 'Love is All', which was very popular in the Netherlands.

So I checked out 'On Stage' in the store. After Judy Garland spoke her words, 'Kill the King' started with a bang from Cozy Powell! Then the Hammond organ told me this sounded a lot like Deep Purple. the vocals kicked in... A very powerful, yet very melodic voice took the song over in a way I never heard before in my life. I just discovered Ronnie James Dio, and from this day on, 'On Stage' became a very important album in my music collection, with a lot of memories attached to it.

Soon after that I bought the album with the track list resembling 'On Stage' the best: 'Ritchie Blackmore's Rainbow'. These studio recorded songs were a bit slower and lacked some of the energy the live versions have, the same flaw with most Deep Purple songs. On the other hand I liked the perfection of the album production wise. Also the up beat tempo present in the songs that are not on 'On Stage', like 'Snake Charmer' and 'Black Sheep of the Family' made me love this record even more. The melancholic 'Self Portrait' spoke to me the most in lyrics.I bought this album on CD together with 'Holy Diver'. In contrast with the at times mellow 'Ritchie Blackmore's Rainbow' album, Dio's heavy debut gave me off course a very different listening experience. Heavy metal was not that alien to me, but me really appreciating it like this was new. I liked what I heard and at the time didn't really thought or cared about which genre it belonged to. As long as there is melody in the songs and the lyrics are understandably sung, I can appreciate metal. Dio fits this category really well. It's from here I added more Dio related CD's to my collection. The magical 'Rising' album absolutely mesmerized me. I remember playing the computer game Tetris while listening to 'Stargazer'. In a way building my own tower on this little LCD screen... I also appreciated 'Dream Evil' after a while for what it is; a great well written record, with a more bombastic touch to it due to the synthesizers. It actually became my favourite Dio album from the 80s, together with 'Holy Diver'. A small culture shock occurred when I added 'Strange Highways' to my collection. The most recent album Ronnie James Dio released at this time. Black Sabbath's 'Dehumanizer' was a record I had to buy because of the same reason; a relatively new release. I soon got used to these heavy albums and nowadays still like playing them. Sometimes I want the lyrics telling me the truth, even if those are cynical and dark. Very often the world is not a beautiful place and those albums reflect that perfectly. All this record collecting happened over a course of a year. The first Ronnie James Dio release that came out since I became a fan was 'Angry Machines'. I love this album since it came out. Years later when I got internet (and my first PC for that matter...) I became aware many people don't like 'Angry Machines'. Even Ronnie James Dio himself had some doubts about it later on. It's heavy, handling with everyday life topics in the lyrics, but still very metaphorically written. And Ronnie's voice sounds especially good on this one, not as screamy anymore as on 'Strange Highways'. And I like the overall thick heavy sound of 'Angry Machines'.

Me living mostly at night at the time -while zapping through channels- Deep Purple caught my attention, on a German music television show called Rockpalast. A concert recorded in 1985 was aired. Ian Gillan had a cold and sadly you could barely hear him singing. After that to my surprise, a Rainbow concert started in! I have this concert on a DVD nowadays, it's called 'Live in Munich 1977', a must have for any Rainbow fan. It was the first time I've ever seen Ronnie James Dio make his legendary dramatic moves. Later on I dreamed about visiting a concert not that big in a park (!), with Ronnie James performing on a stage in this 70s incarnation... Probably me visiting an open-air festival with Aerosmith as a headliner influenced this dream.

In 1997, when I discovered the band Dio came to Amsterdam, I had to go there off course. This event took place in a small venue called Paradiso. It was great seeing Ronnie James Dio performing live. It was the only time I've seen him. A bit to my surprise Dio played mostly older songs, the more recent songs they did were 'Hunter of the Heart' and the best opening song there is 'Jesus, Mary & the Holy Ghost'. From written interviews I learned that Ronnie described himself as someone who cares about his fans. This evening in Paradiso I witnessed this with my own eyes. Between songs someone threw roses to Ronnie from the balcony. A sincere smile followed as answer, he walked off stage (saving the roses) with a funny gallop, holding the roses above his head. Later on this evening Ronnie made worshipping moves with his arms to the audience. It was a great evening. I purchased 'Last in Line', because now I knew the the title track they played live. The last song 'Egypt (The Chains Are On)' became my favourite track of that album. Years later, I played the song and after that I decided to play the other tracks from 8 to 1; ending with 'We Rock'. I do this till this day when I play the 'Last in Line' album, It's one of those things...For a long time I only knew live renditions of Black Sabbath's 'Heaven and Hell'. First the 'Live Evil' version played entirely by a classic rock radio station here in the Netherlands (those were the days...) After that I've seen Dio covering the song on stage in Amsterdam. And before finally buying the wonderful Black Sabbath album 'Heaven and Hell', I had to play the 'Dio's Inferno – The Last in Live' track, to hear the great lyric "The world is full of kings and queens who blind your eyes and steal your dreams". While this beautiful phrase is the most known, it's the less cryptic: "The closer you get to the meaning, the sooner you'll know that you're dreaming" that's even more accurate in describing my life. Nowadays I have found however some peace with the fact I don't know a lot of things...Songs like 'Heaven and Hell' are not only dealing with good vs. bad, for me it's also asking what actually evil is, in this or other worlds, because it can fool you. Not everything is what it appears to be. I like the fatalistic lyrics on his later work too, like on the songs 'Black' or 'End of the World'. Not grotesque like a Hollywood blockbuster about how the world is ending, but from a much more personal perspective; written from personal observations, worrying about the world might stop if everything continues the same way. Now with ten years YouTube, and so many interviews available to watch, I am even more aware of the intelligence Ronnie James Dio had, what a well spoken man he was. He had always something interesting to say in interviews.

The day the news came to me Ronnie James Dio had died was very strange. At first I couldn't get used to it. Then after a few days the reality slowly settled in... Never again the chance to see him live. Never again experience the joy of waiting for a new album, wondering what he will do next, with whom in the band. Never again listening to a new released album for the first time. The last time was with Heaven & Hell. A band that gave us only one great studio album (under this moniker anyway). 'The Devil You Know' became a fitting last act after all.

What I still do waiting for is the release of the biography he was working on, which supposedly will be finished by Wendy Dio. And; while there is already a beautiful statue in Bulgaria, there's a internet petition I signed a few weeks back, to help raise a statue in his birthplace Portsmouth. Ronnie James Dio really deserves this! I hope it will happen.

Machiel Zwart - forever a fan (Netherlands)

ROMANIA

Capital City:	Bucharest
Population:	19,511,000
Currency:	Romanian Leu
Bands:	Negură Bunget, Trooper, Byron

"Forever he will be #1 until I meet him again, every year this hurts. I saw him in Dallas and a consummate crowd lover the best.
Yes my new brother and I think all of us that knew him laid some of ourselves in that coffin with him. After he died I got Cushing's disease and I have been walking dead ever since.
I know some of my health lies with him."
Morkan Vladeslas (Sibiu, Romania)

SINGAPORE

Capital City:	Singapore
Population:	5,535,000
Currency:	Singapore Dollar
Bands:	Stompin' Ground, Impiety, Wormrot

"LONG LIVE ROCK N ROLL.... DIO RAINBOW."
Nazirah Sa'awi (Singapore)

SWITZERLAND

Capital City: Bern
Population: 8,211,700
Currency: Swiss Franc
Bands: Krokus, Gotthard, Celtic Frost, Coroner

"We Rock!"
Aurelio Violante (Geneva, Switzerland)

"So personally I think it's great and I'm the biggest fan of the collaboration between Blackmore and Ronnie and I listen Rainbow on loop since I was 15!!! For me it is one of the most rich and varied rock bands of all time!!
Dio has been for me the first perfect voice and the Heavy class personified."
David aka Big DD (Fribourg, Switzerland)

"I'd like to share my grief with you. It's been really hard to take for me. I loved everything about Ronnie, he was my hero.
As he was diagnosed with cancer, I thought about losing him and that it would never be the same again. After a chemo he'll never be able to do extensive World tours again. The last time I saw the band Dio was in 2003, at the 'Bang Your Head'. Unfortunately, the 'Master of the Moon' Tour never came to Switzerland.
As his work with Sabbath is my favorite music of all time, I was really glad that they reunited and attended all concerts here in Switzerland. I loved 'The Devil You Know' and was amazed that Ronnie still drove on with his own band and did tours. The 2008 and the proposed 2009 Tour, that never happened, didn't include a Swiss date, so I seriously thought about going to Germany to see him.
I tried so much to meet him, since I became a huge fan in 1997, when I discovered him through a friend who pointed out the Spectrum Video at a store to me, I found the 'Diamonds' CD and the very next day I returned and bought the video, through the Songwriting credits I discovered his Rainbow and Sabbath-Past, being a Sabbath Fan already, that made my world so 'round. Remember that was before the Internet and before the encyclopedias. The only source I got was the magazines.

Needless to say I acquired all the back catalogue and found out that that same friend once gave me 'Dehumnanizer', 'cause he didn't like it. I turned around the moment I found out who these Iommi, Butler guys were and held the CD in my hand: That was a revelation!!! As a big Waynes World Fan, I recognized the tune. Only years later, I remembered watching that videoclip with the frog I watched as a kid 'Butterfly Ball'….

One of my first concerts was the 'Angry Machines' Tour. I screamed so loud at the end of the concert that Dio turned around and did point the finger on me. I couldn't attend the 1998 'Inferno' Tour, as we had a concert with my own group Emerald, and the other members had me sell my ticket to the Dio show.

A friend of mine went and brought back a signed booklet of 'Inferno', which read: "To Adriano, all the best, Ronne James Dio". Boy, I treasured that item like the treasure it was.

I attended the 'Magica' tour in 2000, where I took pictures with Craig and got the drumstick, I had caught, signed by Simon. Still no sight of Ronnie, I couldn't meet him. Later the year at the 'Concerto' gigs, obviously I couldn't meet him either. I took my future wife to the 'Killing the Dragon' Tour, where she witnessed his 'greatness' live. She still remembers waiting for Ronnie, but he only waved and went into the bus. Graciously, he allowed 1 item per person to be signed. As you might have guessed I got two…

This year I also went to the 'Bang Your Head' and stood almost front row at the Dio Gig and sang 'Temple of the King' with fellow fans prior to the gig. It gave me a sense of fulfillment when you see other people loving Dio as much as I.

> We will always remember Ronnie, he will always live in our hearts –
> Adriano Troiano

Over the Years 'Dehumanizer' developed into being my favorite record, as it is mean, modern and complex in a sense, that the songs open over time. I listened to 'Computer God' over a 100 times and loved it so much, I always played it when I overcame something in my life (exams…) or when I was home alone. Sadly, I told myself: No way these guys are going to be back together, no band reforms for a second time….there was talk of a Rainbow reunion, but Dio-Sabbath was it for me.

When the 'Best of Dio-Years' came out, I was really excited. The gig at the 'Spirit of Rock' Festival was awesome, I bought almost every T-shirt and was glad that my favorite band has a name of it's own. I even went to Montreux to see them again, where I met Vinny, but no Ronnie. The next time, after 'The Devil You Know' I said make it or break it and contacted everyone I know who could help me meet my hero. And the Dio Fanclub did it for me, It could have worked earlier, but until the moment they handed my the aftershow pass I just couldn't believe it.

I took everything with me and had the pleasure to meet him in Person, a dream of myself came through. I bought a frog to give to him and took pictures. He was kind enough to sign all of my collection. I remember it vividly and was happier than ever. This was a gig at the Volkshaus (has nothing to do with the 'Spirit of Rock', btw). There was that little episode, where I was sitting there in his dressing room and my eyes wandered around, I was in awe and Ronnie caught my eyes and gave me the sign, I guess he knew that I was living the dream.

The day after the concert I wrote a song about that experience. I just recently (two weeks ago) looked at that song again and played it to find out, it's really great and that I'm going to put it on my next album with my project Distant Past. After all, I started writing lyrics and wanting to be in a band because of my love for Dio. I wanted the song to sound like Sabbath, but somehow it sounds like Candlemass. I will record it in the future, for now I only have sung it with my guitar.

We will always remember Ronnie, he will always live in our hearts."

Adriano Troiano (Bern, Switzerland)

Dio

'Killing the Dragon' Tour
Z7 Konzertfabrik, Pratteln, Switzerland
21st September 2002

Killing the Dragon
Egypt (The Chains Are On)
Children of the Sea
Push
Stand Up and Shout
Rock and Roll
Don't Talk to Strangers
Man on the Silver Mountain
Long Live Rock 'n' Roll
Lord of the Last Day
Fever Dreams
The Mob Rules
Holy Diver
Heaven and Hell
The Last in Line
Rainbow in the Dark
We Rock

United Arab Emirates

Capital City: Abu Dhabi
Population: 5,779,760
Currency: UAE Dirham
Bands: Nikotin, Tsvet Reptilia, E.Y.E., The Boxtones

"RJD changed me. When I first saw his first video, and THEN learned that he was previously in Rainbow and Sabbath, I knew this voice and lyrics were somehow speaking to me.
(I must have been living in a cave for not knowing about the previous bands)
Since that first day listening to 'The Last in Line'... I've not been the same, and have never faltered in the fact he was and is my favorite singer ever. Luckily, I saw many tours of Dio and Heaven and Hell."
Jon Bush (Dubai, United Arab Emirates)

UNITED KINGDOM

Capital City: London
Population: 64,716,000
Currency: Pound Sterling
Bands: Black Sabbath, Iron Maiden, Judas Priest

*"I loved Ronnie.
I can't remember what year I saw him at Donington, but it must have been an early one. I think, if we had met, we would have got on.
He had a fabulous voice, and I used to think he wouldn't have been out of place in The Lord of The Rings.
Where Lemmy was my Shenanigator, my outlet, Ronnie was the warm blanket, the hug, and the storyteller in my miserable childhood. I still miss him."*
Karen Whaley (Derby)

*"I never met Ronnie. But I remember buying 'Rainbow Rising' when it came out coz it had a cool cover. Wow.
One of my all time heroes. Went on to collect every album he was on. Even just for one song.
Saw him with Sabbath a few times and solo with Dio lots. Still miss him."*
Roger Dighton (Milton Keynes)

*"I used to work at Bristol Colston Hall on the security and I'll never forget what a great bunch Dio were.
After a brilliant gig, the head of security asked a couple of us if we'd stay on after the show, as the band would come out and meet the fans. Surely enough, we let about 50 fans who were waiting outside at the stage door back into the venue, sat them in the stalls at the back and Ronnie and the band came out and met everyone.
I'll never forget how happy they all were, to have photos taken, sign autographs and chat to their fans, I don't remember many other bands going out of their way to do this.
Great memories, and a great man. God bless Ronnie James Dio, Jimmy Bain, Viv Campbell and Vinny Appice, you made people happy, and you rocked!"*
Dave Tansley (Portishead, Somerset)

'Holy Diver' Tour
Colston Hall, Bristol
31st October 1983

Stand Up and Shout
Straight Through the Heart
Shame on the Night
Children of the Sea
Holy Diver
Stargazer
Heaven and Hell
Rainbow in the Dark
Man on the Silver Mountain / Starstruck
Evil Eyes
Don't Talk to Strangers

I've been a Dio fan since around 1982 firstly with his work in Sabbath and the Dio the band.
I went to see them on the 'Lock Up the Wolves' tour & decided to hang about in the afternoon to see if I could meet them. It was a horrible day and the tour manager took pity on me and gave me a backstage pass to meet the band afterwards.
Dio perfomed a great gig, unfortunately I tried to be a fly-boy & get my mate Slim backstage as well on my pass. The bouncer was having none of it and took my pass off me. Depressed we decided to still wait to meet the band. When Ronnie and the boys came out we got some stuff signed & took some photos including my mate Colin who idolised Ronnie and still does.
The manager even gave me back the backstage pass, which I got signed. After the disappointment of having my pass taken off me it all turned good. There'll never be another voice in rock as good as Dio's RIP RJD."

Gary Begg (Wick, Scotland)

"My memories of Ronnie would be his voice. Miss him so much."
Sarah Harris (Chichester)

"Ronnie slays man, true King."
Rio Green (Sittingbourne, Kent)

"RONNIE JAMES DIO...the ELF with the voice of thunder...when you RUN WITH THE WOLF in search of the SACRED HEART...along the hidden road you'll find the ROCK AND ROLL CHILDREN pointing to the stars where the STARGAZER sits waiting to CATCH THE RAINBOW.... yo"
Edinson Restrepo Alizandre (London)

"I liked him in Black Sabbath."
Kim Bradley (Newcastle Upon Tyne)

"I remember Dio as a figure head in Heaven and Hell when he took over from Ozzy Osbourne and the seeing him in the film 'Tenacious D – The Pick of Destiny.
But the first I heard of him was when Killswitch Engage covered his song Holy Diver."
Jonnie Allman (Handforth, Cheshire)

"I've seen him many times, but never met him.
My favorite time was on the Heaven and Hell 2007 reunion tour, the power coming out of that voice still blew me away. For a little guy, he had the lungs of Goliath. Never dropped or faultered a note, simply the greatest metal vocalist there is, was and ever will be. His legacy speaks volumes."
Simon Turner (Newport)

"I started listening to Dio when I was fifteen; the first album I listened to was 'Rising', the one he did vocals for with Ritchie Blackmore's Rainbow, and the track was 'Stargazer'. It was eight minutes of pure hard rock pleasure, and something I would never forget for the rest of my life. I knew I was going down to the record store to buy the record, even though at the time they were really hard to get, and considered retro. But luckily I managed to pick up a mint condition copy of it for just £8 – what a bargain considering at the time it was nearly thirty-nine years old!

My love affair with Dio didn't stop there. I moved on from Rainbow and onto the likes of Black Sabbath, which I'd become hooked on 'Mob Rules' and 'Heaven & Hell', I just didn't know who the singer was, until I heard Rainbow, and it clicked that it was the same powerful, gravelly voice that sang the vocals on 'Long Live Rock 'n' Roll'. 'Neon Knights' became my favourite track alongside 'Holy Diver', which he did with his solo group; it's what I, as an eclectic music fan would say, a true heavy metal anthem. The video is packed full of action, leaving you wondering what happens to him in the end.

Every fan that I have met through the internet or fan forums, are the high envy of me, either because they have had the privilege of meeting him or seeing him live, whether he was backed by Rainbow or Sabbath. The only regret I have is that I wasn't born in time to see him perform whilst he was still alive, but like I always say, thank heavens for YouTube and Vimeo, many fans have uploaded their precious memories of the legend, a true god of metal.

Ronnie James Dio will go down in the history books as one of the pioneers of heavy metal and rock; no one can replace him, not even Rainbow's new front man, Ronnie Romero. My goal is to visit his plaque on the Hollywood Walk of Fame, as after all, he truly deserved it.

Horns up, Dio. May you rest in peace."
Megan Taylor Ure (Barnsley)

"I haven't met Dio person but I liked the big strong voice for such a tiny rock legend. Powerful voice.
I liked Black Sabbath with Dio with them, Heaven and Hell and many more and when he did his own stuff as Dio and with Rainbow. I would've loved to have been to his concerts but never did.
R I P DIO. Long Live Rock and Roll.
My Son Adam loves him also."
Kim Bradley (Newcastle upon Tyne)

"I went to see Deep Purple on their 1974 'Burn' tour at Newcastle Odeon in the UK.
The support band came on and this tiny bloke stepped up to the mic.
I thought "Who the hell is that?"
When he opened his mouth I thought "You're gonna reach the stars."

The band were Elf and Ronnie James Dio gave the best vocal performance I have ever been privileged to see. Everything - His stagecraft, the lot, was Fantastic.
Shortly afterwards that band minus their guitarist became Ritchie Blackmore's Rainbow and the 1st Rainbow album - to me - is still classic Rainbow.
Only one regret is that I never saw Ronnie perform again, but my memories of that May night still burn (no pun intended) brightly."
Keith Markham (Berwick-Upon-Tweed)

"I am a very good friend of Geoff Nicholls who was in the band QUARTZ but left to help his good friend Tony Iommi in the Summer of 1979 following the sacking of Ozzy Osbourne etc.
Geoff was only supposed to be away for a few weeks but actually ended up staying nearly 24 years.
Obviously Geoff was there at the start when Ronnie came on board for 'Heaven and Hell' LP and 'Mob Rules' LP and again when he returned for 'Dehumaniser'.
Geoff kindly got my Heaven and Hell tour program signed for me when they played the Birmingham Odeon."
Tim Perry (Oldbury, West Midlands)

"Ronnie was the first rocker to use the devils horn sign and would never comprise his sword and sorcery lyrics.
Songs such as 'Stargazer', 'The Sign Of The Southern Cross' and 'Holy Diver' showed his charisma and vocal range.
Whatever band Ronnie fronted he made his mark.
I never tire of listening to his style."
Doug Earle (Liverpool)

"1980: East Westfalia Halle, Germany, 'Heaven and Hell' tour.
I was in the army stationed at Lippstadt so when we heard Black Sabbath were playing in the town of Verl half a dozen of us got tickets.
If I'm right I think it was Ronnie's third live appearance with Sabbath.
I have been to hundreds of concerts throughout my life but that one stands heads above any other. Still can remember the volume of the band hammering our bodies but Ronnie's vocals were so clear and precise.
A magical man, a legend. RIP Ronnie James Dio."
James McKinnon (Clydebank, Scotland)

"First time I heard him was in Rainbow. I was in my teens and 'Rising' was one of the first LP's I bought on vinyl. Still one of my favourite albums of all time, nearly 40 years later."
Soraya Hekattee Rojas (Worksop)

"I have great memories of Ronnie going way back and seeing the promo clip for 'BUTTERFLY BALL' on TV in the 1970's, been a fan ever since.
Finally got to see the great man in 1987 at Donington, where he truly delivered the goods with his fantastic band. I managed to get his attention for a second where I got his trademark horn salute and a big smile from him, which made my day.
Sadly, I never got to meet him. My friend Steve did a few years ago and Ronnie very kindly signed his autograph for me, saying "TO MARTIN "MAGIC" RONNIE JAMES DIO". It says a lot about Ronnie that he took the time to do that for someone who wasn't even there when he signed it. I will treasure it always.
Ronnie James Dio was a first class musician who took us to wonderful worlds with his music and more importantly he really appreciated his fans and did everything he could to make us happy.
A rock icon and a true gentleman.
We miss you Ronnie.
Thanks for the memories.
Martin Evans (Llanelli, Wales)

"I'm glad in a way I was born 10 days early as he would of died on what of been my 21st and that would of been a sad birthday and would of been associated with all round sadness as it happens it wasn't but still sad and he is still sadly missed RIP Ronnie James dio (originally Padavona)"
Jade Forster (Blackpool)

"Where has the last 6 years gone?
Every time I see a rainbow I can't help thinking of his amazing vocals and the pleasure I still get from his music. I am so glad I got to see him perform live on so many occasions.
Long Live Rock 'n' Roll! And Rock In Peace!"
Mick Brown (Radlett, UK)

"A group of us were concert goers in the 70s. We went to the Liverpool Stadium and later the Empire.

In Nov '77 we saw Rainbow at the Empire. There was this guy on stage; it was Ronnie James Dio of course striding the stage like a giant. A rounded powerful voice competing with Ritchie Blackmore with his talent and charisma. Great concert - Great artist."
Doug Earle (Liverpool)

Rainbow

'Rising' Tour
Empire Theatre Liverpool
5th November '77

Kill the King
Mistreated
Sixteenth Century Greensleeves
Catch the Rainbow
Long Live Rock 'n' Roll
Man on the Silver Mountain
Still I'm Sad
Do You Close Your Eyes

"I always think of Dio as the little gentleman in black velvet. I was lucky enough to see him four times.
I first saw him at Wembley, with Alice Cooper in 2001, and was impressed by the power of his voice and his agility as he ran about the stage, making sure everyone got a look at him.
I also saw him at the smaller Astoria in London in 2002.
I saw him at the Brighton Centre in 2007 on the Heaven and Hell tour and it was a wonderful atmosphere, with a whole age range of people, young teenage fans and older fans in their sixties and beyond.
I last saw him at Wacken in 2009, again with Heaven and Hell. The whole crowd sang along and I even saw a man having a wee in time to the music.
RJD is remembered fondly in many ways; every time someone throws the horns, that's his legacy in action.
I also like his memorial brick at the Wacken Open Air festival.
Sarah Tipper (England)

Heaven and Hell
'Bible Black' Tour
Wacken Open Air Festival
30th July 2009

The Mob Rules
Children of the Sea
I
Bible Black
Time Machine
Fear
Falling Off the Edge of the World
Follow the Tears
Die Young
Heaven and Hell
Country Girl
Neon Knights

*"Ronnie James Dio was, is and will be rock n' roll. His legacy will live on forever and ever.....
Long live rock 'n' roll!.. Long live Ronnie James Dio!
The most awesome and wonderful Man on the Silver Mountain."*
Angela Perado (London)

*"Myself and my friend had been invited to the show through Doug Aldrich (whom we knew through Whitesnake) who had taken on guitar work or Ronnie since Craig Goldy had injured his hand.
The show was of course fantastic and the band stormed the venue. After the show we went backstage and chatted in the corridor to Doug and the rest of the band (Simon Wright, Rudy Sarzo and Scott Warren).
Dio was in the green room chatting to some other celebs that had been there (including Tony Iommi).
Doug went to get a shower and the others were mixing in the green room. We just stood about awkwardly in the corridor too frightened to disturb Dio. Wendy came out and asked if everything was okay Ronnie had seen us and was wondering why we hadn't gone in. We explained our fears and she smiled.
A couple of minutes later Dio came out and asked us why the fuck we didn't have a beer and invited us into the room. We stumbled in and he introduced himself to us both (like we didn't know who he was!!) and went straight to the fridge and got us a beer each telling us to help ourselves (Dio got us beer !!) He asked if we had enjoyed the show and was genuinely happy and greatful with our response.
I asked him about various albums and we chatted for a long time, no looking at his watch or looking around getting bored. I have never met a man so genuine in my life.*

After a couple of hours Wendy came in and announced it was time for the band to go as they had to be in London for the recording of the new DVD and they had a lot to do the next day. Ronnie shook our hands again and told us what a pleasure it was to have a chat and a beer with us and it's fans like us that makes the job worthwhile.

Shaking our hands again and thanking us he then invited us down to the London show the next night as his guests!!! How could we refuse??

Fantastic couple of nights with such a gentleman."

Dan Thomason (Hesswal, Wirral)

Dio

'Holy Diver – Anniversary Tour
Birmingham Academy
27th May '08

Holy Diver
Killing the Dragon
The Eyes
Don't Talk to Strangers
Sacred Heart
Rainbow in the Dark
The Temple of the King
Kill the King
Lord of the Last Day
Rock 'n' Roll Children
Stand Up and Shout
Man on the Silver Mountain
Catch the Rainbow
Long Live Rock 'n' Roll
The Last in Line
We Rock

"I was lucky enough to be at the 'An Evening With Dio' UK tour at Exeter University in 2005. They played two sets. The first was a collection of classics from Dio's back catalogue and the second was the whole of 'Holy Diver'.
What an incredible night. RIP Mr Ronnie James...."
Mike Horton (Plymouth)

"The only memorial I have of Dio - Heaven Thru Hell memorial tattoo not finished yet."
Manolo Satanas Rojas (Worksop)

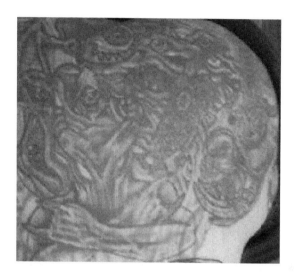

"The first time I heard Ronnie James Dio sing was on a Black Sabbath compilation called 'Blackest Sabbath' nearly 30 years ago, the live version of 'Children of the Sea' (off the "Live Evil' album) is my favourite live song from any live album ever.
I'm a massive Sabbath fan and love all eras of Sabbath but I've always had a particular love for the Iommi, Dio, Butler, Appice line up. I never forget buying a copy of Kerrang! a couple of years later and reading that Dio was back in Sabbath, and the album that followed - 'Dehumanizer' - is one of my all time favourite albums. They were due to play in Dublin on that tour but for some reason the gig was cancelled, of all the gigs I've had cancelled over the years, that is the one I would have most like to have seen.
Anyway roll on thirteen years because on the 25th of October 2005, Dio and his band did roll into Dublin to play a sold out gig in the Ambassador Theatre and sang the 'Holy Diver' album in its entirety along with Rainbow, Sabbath and other Dio era classics. All I can say about seeing Ronnie on stage for the first time is it

was a night of pure metal magic, Ronnie's stage presence along with his majestic voice and gratitude toward the fans is an experience that will stay with me forever.

Never in my wildest dreams did I believe that I would get to see him onstage with Iommi, Butler and Appice so when I heard they were reforming Sabbath under the Heaven and Hell name, I was the happiest metal fan alive and got to them live in the Allstate Arena in Chicago on the 5th of May and again in London Wembley Arena on the 10th of November '07. So fifteen years after the disappointment of the Dublin cancellation I got to see my favourite singer singing with my all time favourite band for not one but two nights of pure heavy metal majesty at its very, very best.

Sadly the Wembley show was the last time I got to see Dio. I had tickets, flights and hotel booked for myself and my then 10 year old son for the Dio tour in '09 in Manchester but sadly the cancer diagnosis meant it wasn't to be.

Since Dio's passing I was lucky enough to be able to attend the Heaven and Hell tribute to Dio at the High Voltage festival, and have also seen the Dio Disciples and Last in Line play live and while all their respective singers did a fantastic job, there will never be anybody able to replace the sheer magic of the greatest heavy metal singer of all time, his legend and his music will live forever."

Peter Morrissey (Rathdrum, Wicklow)

"The man the myth the legend Dio forever in our hearts."
Graeme Thomson (Whitburn, West Lothian)

"My first memory of him was the Tommy Vance show around 84/85. He played 'Man on the Silver Mountain' at the beginning of his show and I was completely taken aback by Ronnie's voice.

Then it was all about trawling through record fairs to find anything he'd sang on.

I'd say my favourite 'live' memory is of him at Sonisphere with Heaven and Hell, it was obvious he wasn't in the best of health but he didn't let that effect him. Me and my buddy's cried all the way through the show because we had a feeling it might be the last chance we'd see him again.

Another sad but great memory of mine is listening to Heaven and Hell in my big brothers car just a few weeks before he got killed in a bike crash back in 2003. My bruv was a huge fan of anything Dio as well and I always raise a glass and take some time out whenever I hear anything off that album."

Paul O'Hare (Liverpool)

Heaven and Hell

Sonisphere Festival
Knebworth Park

The Mob Rules
Children of the Sea
I
Bible Black
Time Machine
Fear
Falling Off the Edge of the World
Die Young
Heaven and Hell

"My memories of metal and rock in my youth are all there. It was the early eighties when I first heard of Ronnie James Dio. I'm forty-five born on the 2nd of December 1970. I've never seen Ronnie James Dio in concert, I would've in 2010 at the 02 in Dublin when Heaven and Hell were billed to support Iron Maiden but Ronnie had died of cancer.

I used to buy second hand records and new ones when I was in my early teens I remember buying 'Live Evil' by Black Sabbath, 'Heaven and Hell' by Black Sabbath and Rainbow 'Long Live Rock n' Roll.

Amongst other things, 'Holy Diver' which was condemned as 'satanic', as a matter of fact most of my record collection was seen as that and the reason I was able to buy second hand records from school friends is their parents gave off stink to them and demanded they get rid of 'that satanic muck' out of their house! I remember "The Last In Line', 'Don't Talk to Strangers', 'Rainbow in the Dark', they were brand new when I bought them. 7" singles, watching Top of the Pops was something I always looked forward to on a Thursday night on BBC1 and the anticipation in me waiting for the greatest musical genre of all time, heavy metal and rock actually. W.A.S.P. had a video similar to one Ronnie James Dio did with that glass globe with the electricity going to the point of human contact! I watched the charts for them all - Thin Lizzy, Twisted Sister, Whitesnake, Iron Maiden and even Slade had

some good stuff out in the early eighties.
Larry Gogan on RTE2 radio had a chart show and I used to make compilations from the chart show buying ten blank audiocassettes in a pack. Dio featured heavily back then, mainstream rock/metal. Dave Fanning from 2 FM also back then was a great champion of rock and metal, in 1984 he did an interview with Ronnie, Vivian Campbell, Vinny Appice, were in Dio at the time and Ronnie spoke at length about them and the band. There were three interviews that night one after the other, and Philip Lynott was one of them, Grand Slam with Phil were on the go and I remember '19' being one of the songs played.
I'm a fan of so many rockers and Ronnie James Dio is one of the best of them. The esoteric nature of not only of Ronnie's lyrics and the art of the Dio album covers, but of all in the rock business is fantastic, brilliant. And as a rocker I know. I've lived that life where the experiences of those that were there as we passed through time went through. And that is nothing to be sniffed at. Serious stuff and also it shows how god protects us all.
As we go through time we enter and exit different supernatural states, sometimes madness, sometimes holiness, and then there's sin and grace, our goal is heaven, it doesn't mean there has to be a sterile squeaky clean life because we are all human, god helps all of us, in our music our writing our singing, and I believe Ronnie James Dio was a man of faith. Rock n' roll baby! Long live Ronnie."
Jim Chapman (London)

"R.I.P Ronnie an unforgetable mighty voice."
Angela Young (Wallasey)

"LEGEND!"
Gary Pardoe (Pontypridd)

"Was fortunate enough to see the great man with Rainbow, Black Sabbath, Dio and Heaven and Hell. His songwriting skills and vocal lyrics will in my opinion never ever be beaten. Rest In Peace, The Man On The Silver Mountain. Gone, but never forgotten."
Robert Good (UK)

"Loved Dio saw him in Liverpool with Sabbath on the Heaven and Hell tour.. Great voice, sadly missed. ♥"
Des Rimmer (St Helens, Merseyside)

"First saw Dio in Rainbow at Liverpool '77, then in Sabbath and god knows how many times in Dio, including at Donington. For me his best times were Rainbow, but a matter of opinion I guess? Had a ticket for Dio's Manchester show, but it was cancelled due to the saddess.
Long live rock 'n' roll..."
Paul Diable (Weston, Cheshire)

Rainbow

**'Rising' Tour
Empire Theatre,
Liverpool
5th November 1977**

**Kill the King
Mistreated
Sixteenth Century Greensleeves
Catch the Rainbow
Long Live Rock 'n' Roll
Man on the Silver Mountain
Still I'm Sad
Do You Close Your Eyes**

"The thing I remember the most about the gig at Newcastle City Hall in 1976 as you must take into consideration that the bottles of Newcastle Brown Ale served at the nearby pre drinks Man in the Moon pub were always a powerful Geordie potion!!!...Was the

overriding arch above the stage that constituted the rainbow...that signified that Rainbow were about to take the stage.
As the band took to the stage the rainbow was lit up and created a wondrous frame for the band to perform.... somewhere during the set there was some interference coming through the PA system.... must have been the high wattage to power the darn thing.... good job then the band were not called Richie Blackmore's Double Rainbow!!! As I think they might have short-circuited the whole city never mind the stage prop!!!...."
Ian Luck (Saltburn-by-the-Sea)

"Ronnie James Dio. Where do I start. It could only be this. If not the greatest heavy rock/metal vocalists of all time, he is one of them. Three of the greatest rock/metal albums ever, that is not chance. 'Rainbow Rising' – 'Heaven and Hell' – 'Holy Diver' (not that the likes of 'Long Live Rock 'n' Roll' – 'Mob Rules' and 'Last in Line' were a dip in quality). He proved it time and time again
Right live. I only had the pleasure of seeing him live twice. Once in the guise of Heaven and Hell and another time touring under his own name. Simply two awesome gigs. These were both in the latter part of his career, He had looked after his voice. It really looked like the whole band was enjoying themselves when Heaven and Hell played Plymouth. The solo Dio gig was in Southampton and again it was a storming gig. Everything points towards him being a gentlemen onstage and in interviews.
I bear him no ill will despite not playing "Stargazer" no matter how many times I screamed it at the stage, the guy was class
Dio was so good live, one of my friends (Simon) travelled near 3 hrs to see him play here (Plymouth) and I did the same journey in the other direction to see he play the other time.
Simply put Ronnie James Dio – Legend."
Liam Kelly (Plymouth, Devon)

'Holy Diver Live' Tour
Exeter University
Great Hall
17th October '05

Tarot Woman
The Sign of the Southern Cross
One Night in the City
Stand Up and Shout
Holy Diver
Gypsy
Caught in the Middle
Don't Talk to Strangers
Straight Through the Heart
Invisible
Rainbow in the Dark
Shame on the Night
Gates of Babylon
Heaven and Hell
Man on the Silver Mountain
Catch the Rainbow
Long Live Rock 'n' Roll
The Last in Line
We Rock

"Ah, dear Ronnie. I remember buying Dream Evil when it came out and being totally captivated with the songs therein. It was the beginning of a long (still is) standing appreciation of the man and his music, which got even better when I saw him twice in the early 2000's in London, and also on the last two Heaven And Hell gigs in the UK. I was extremely sad when he passed away, but, more than ever, I listen to his music and think, my goodness, we were lucky to hear him for all that while."
Craigie Storey (Newbury, Berkshire)

"Today is Monday 16th of May 2016, and on this day six years ago I read the bad news that Ronnie James Dio had died from cancer. I know in a few days time it will also be exactly fifteen years since I last saw him performing live, in fact it will be fifteen years since I saw anyone performing live. Once I got into Heavy Metal I fell in love with the classics Motorhead, Dio, AC/DC, Black Sabbath, Iron Maiden etc. and would see them whenever they were playing in London. I also followed the new groups and touring groups on the scene, with favourites like Orange Goblin, Iron Monkey, Spin Pit, Pulkas, T.B.A.C. and Medulla Nocte.

Having moved to Norfolk from West London in 1999 I had not been to many gigs in the previous year so when I saw that in May 2001 Alice Cooper was headlining at Wembley Arena with Dio supporting it was a no brainer, I booked my ticket and then was over the moon when I found that my old mates Orange Goblin, who I had followed, and drunk with, since they were Our Haunted Kingdom, were now booked to open!

When the day arrived I got to Wembley early so I could get a few in at the traditional meeting point for all Wembley gigs, The Green Man on Dagmar Avenue, and also so I didn't miss Orange Goblin's slot which started really early, at 18:30. Having seen them play at pubs and clubs all over London, quite often with them putting my name on the door, it was amazing to see them playing on such a large stage, especially knowing who was going to be playing on it after them, and who they were backstage with!

Orange Goblin put out quite a short set for them, and as they were onstage so early, with most of the fans not expecting an early start or third group performing, a lot of people missed their set, which was a shame as hearing their tracks blasting out was a treat, and showed that Ben was suited to a stage where he had more room to move, and that Joe could still be seen from a distance!

Then came the Main act for me, Don't get me wrong, I love Alice Cooper, but I had already seen him half a dozen times in the previous years, as I had with Dio (albeit in various forms) but it was Dio I was really there to see!

The tension in Wembley was palpable as it seemed many like me felt Dio was the headline act that night and finally on he came, after the usual teasing build up, opening the set with Sunset Superman from the 'Dream Evil' LP, surely one of the best show openers ever, and the place erupted!

This was followed by Invisible, from the first Dio solo album I bought, 'Holy Diver', which was one of Thirteen tracks he played that night, 'Holy Diver', a personal favourite came nearer the end and he closed with 'We Rock'. Dio was on form that night, and I still reckon that it was the best performance I had ever seen from him! At the end of the set I almost forgot we still had Alice Cooper to come!

Alice Cooper then proceeded to do a mammoth set, opening with Brutal Planet he managed 28 numbers including Two encores, made even better by realising that Brian May had joined the stage for a minute of 'We Will Rock You' before staying and joining in on 'School's Out'!

All in all an extremely memorable night with three fantastic sets! Made all the more memorable for me as it was the last gig I was ever able to get to and see, having been to over 300 gigs by then, as five months later I collapsed whilst at work and have been disabled ever since.

I may not have been able to go to a gig for 15 years now, or seen any of my old friends perform, or any of my favourite acts perform, but at least the last gig I ever managed to get to was such an amazing one, and one which for many reasons I will never forget!

Skull Gutteridge (UK)

'Magica' Tour – Supporting Alice Cooper
Wembley Arena, London
18th May '01

Sunset Superman
Invisible
Stand Up and Shout
Don't Talk to Strangers
Wild One
Magica Theme
Lord of the Last Day
Fever Dreams
Holy Diver
Heaven and Hell
Man on the Silver Mountain / Long Live Rock 'n' Roll
The Last in Line
We Rock

Shaun Mayer (Liverpool)

"I guess I first came across Ronnie James Dio back in 1983 when I heard the First Album by the band Dio.
The album 'Holy Diver' is still one of my favourites.
I used to hang around with a group of lads from around 1980 and got into rock music as they bought all the albums and we all used to go around each others houses to listen. We also went to all the rock concerts at the Cornwall Coliseum and Dio was one of those concerts.
I remember back then this guy has an amazing voice but he's so small. As time progressed I realised he had been the singer on my favourite album of all time 'Heaven and Hell' and then the singer with Rainbow. Its funny because I always thought the original Rainbow was the 'Since You've Been Gone' line-up. But when you hear 'Man on the Silver Mountain' it's clear it was a different singer.
I eventually got to see Dio for the last time at Plymouth Pavilions with the old Sabbath lineup Heaven and Hell. I think Ronnie was around 65 but his voice had not deteriorated like so many other singers he was simply amazing.
When he passed on I was devastated and shocked especially as my own mother had passed two days before from cancer also.

Dio will always be my favourite rock singer....The Man on the Silver Mountain."
Linda Mitchell (Plymouth)

'The Last in Line' Tour
Cornwall Coliseum, St Austell
15th September 1984

Stand Up and Shout
One Night in the City
Don't Talk to Strangers
Mystery
Egypt (The Chains Are On)
Holy Diver
Heavene and Hell / The Last in Line
Rainbow in the Dark
Man on the Silver Mountain / Long Live Rock 'n' Roll
We Rock
The Mob Rules

"Remember the first time I met Ronnie James Dio was backstage at Nottingham Royal Centre in the UK.
Standing outside with several album covers (remember those), and as I waited in line to meet one of my heroes, one of the security guys said 'you have too many albums, one signature only'. Dio then looked up and said "Hey he bought my albums I will be signing them", which he did.
That was a great experience and one I will never forget. Over the years I met him many more times seeing him on every UK tour.
A legend and a true gentlemen. Still have those albums of course and always brings back fond memories. Long live rock 'n' roll."
Stuart Brown, Kilburn, Belper, UK.

"Here's a hand engraving I did a few years ago on black glass, from Ritchie Blackmore's Rainbow album cover!!"
Paul Diable (Weston, Cheshire)

"As a life long Ronnie Dio fan I thought I would share my very first meeting with the great man himself.
It was on the 'Holy Diver' tour at the Colston Hall in Bristol that I first had the honour and privilege of meeting the greatest rock

vocalist of all time.
I had walked to the gig with a good friend of mine, Chris Harris, as we wanted to save our cash to buy a tour program.
I was carrying with me the inner Sleeve of the 'Holy Diver' album, which I had carefully cut open so that I could (I hoped) get Ronnie to sign it without ruining the photos.
After an amazing gig a small group of us waited patiently in the hall hoping that the great man would come out and meet us.
We were not disappointed! Ronnie did indeed come out and talked happily with everyone as he signed Jackets and programs etc.
I was talking a little way away to Viv Campbell who was sat off to the back, when my mate Chris called out saying Ronnie wanted a word.
Amazed I quickly made my way over to where Ronnie was standing and he waved the album inner sleeve at me (my mate was trying to get it signed for me as I was to shy to speak to him) telling me off jokingly for reckons his album inner!
He signed the sleeve (as did the rest of the band) and I told him that as a photographer, I didn't want to ruin the pictures so wanted to get the inside signed.
He was then, and always, a perfect gentleman.
I saw him last at the O2 Academy in Bristol and again this was a night to remember.
RIP The greatest Rock/Metal vocalist this planet has ever seen, love you Ronnie!"
Richard Tippett (Bristol)

"First time I saw Ronnie in concert was with Black Sabbath at Newcastle City Hall on the 'Heaven and Hell' tour 1980.
There were quite a few die hard Ozzy fans in the audience who shouted 'Ozzy' ,but RJD had won them over before the third song.
My regret I never got to see Ronnie play live with Rainbow."
Raymond Dixon (Carlisle, Cumbria)

UNITED STATES OF AMERICA

Capital City: Washington D.C.
Population: 322,369,319
Currency: United States Dollar
Bands: Dio, Metallica, Anthrax, KISS

*"I got to see Ronnie on the last Heaven and Hell tour.
My friend Nigel Paul, was doing sound, and we were having a bite to eat in the green room. Ronnie came by to say hi! What a lovely man and great talent, gone far too soon!"*
Debbie Stewart (Urbana, Illinois)

*"My friend played in a band and told me about the time they had just heard that he had passed. It was breaking news on the radio. They were about to go on stage and the band all of whom were HUGE fans were so shocked and almost too grief stricken to play so 2 minutes before getting on stage and without any rehearsal, they played a RJD song, they played it flawless and had a great response.
An overwhelming response from a sold out venue."*
Len Stray (Whittier, California)

*"Ronnie James Dio was the voice of music for me my entire life. It was Rainbow's 'Man on the Silver Mountain' then Sabbath's 'Heaven and Hell'. Next came Dio's 'Holy Diver'.
Later in 2006 I was at George Lynch's wedding in Pioneer Town California. I was talking to Vinnie Appice and he was telling me about "Heaven and Hell" and that Album and Tour was in the works for the following year."*
Shawn Eric Forsberg (Huntingdon Beach, California)

"I have vivid dreams about Ronnie..I'd like to believe he visits me. I love and miss Him terribly. Oh how I miss Him terribly, a fan and a friend forever. He is loved immensely..."
Lisa Fury (Chicago, Illinois)

"I've met Ronnie James Dio on several occasions and he was always the same even during his last days when I was last with him during the Heaven & Hell tour in Atlantic city N.J.
A kind gentle man with a voice as big as the planet and a heart even bigger. Thanks to Adam Parsons and Jethro Hirsch I had these pleasures of being around Ronnie James Dio backstage, autograph sessions and his shows. When he would come out to the many autograph sessions and backstage areas after the show that I've had the pleasure of being at people would go absolutely crazy yelling "Dio, Dio, Dio" and in a calm subtle voice he would say, "calm down everyone I will sign and take all the pictures you would like no problem", what a gem!
There was this instance where I was backstage with Iron Maiden, Dio & MotörHead, thanks to Adam Parsons & I was with Jethro Hirsch and we were taking pictures with Ronnie Dio after the show in the backstage area and Jethro Hirsch scooped up Ronnie Dio in a baby kinda cradle and I yelled at him saying "put Dio down Jethro" and in a subtle voice Dio said
"It's ok TattooTommy, take the picture."
What a beautiful all around person that I'm grateful and honored to have had the pleasure of meeting and being around as often as I was.
Cheers Ronnie James Dio and may your soul rest in peace and I can only hope I will be able to meet up with you in the after life, as well as all our other friends who have passed too."

Thomas 'TattooTommy' Beerman (New Jersey)

Heaven and Hell

**'Bible Black Tour
House of Blues, Atlantic City, NJ
29th August '09**

The Mob Rules
Children of the Sea
I
Bible Black
Time Machine
Fear
Falling Off the Edge of the World
Follow the Tears
Die Young
Heaven and Hell
Country Girl
Neon Knights

"I first met Ronnie at Foundations Forum in 1992. We sat around for over an hour talking about life and music I made a great friend that day the next year at Foundations Forum in 1993 I was standing in line at the bottom of the escalator waiting to go up to talk to Ronnie and Vinnie, Ronnie was up top and saw me down stairs and asked what are you doing down there I said the security wont let me up stairs yet Ronnie talked to security and they let me go up while everyone else in line had to wait.

Ronnie Vinnie and I sat and had coffee and donuts and talked for a long time then Ronnie gave me a Black Sabbath shirt that has the words in red it was the only one like it all the others had the words in white I still have that shirt probably my fondest memory of Ronnie.

Over the years I saw and talked to Ronnie many times what a great guy of all my friends in the music industry that have passed away I miss him the most. The last time I saw Ronnie was on the 'Magica' tour in Amarillo Texas after the show I hung out with Ronnie and Craig until they had to get on the bus and leave. My wife at the time when she met Ronnie asked if he could sign a picture for her son Ronnie said sure and asked his name then after the signing he talked to her for a while about his kid and her kids I will never forget Ronnie what a great gentleman and awesome musician."

Daryl Banks (Jay, Oklahoma)

"My very first concert. One of the best commentaries I ever saw, explained whilst most bands were trying to be the cool party kid, that may or may not be there for you, Dio was looking like the understanding, wise uncle who understood and offered guidance without trying to act like he was still a kid."

Jeannine Haitch (USA)

"I did meet Dio briefly backstage in Concord, as Lemmy's guest. He seemed totally sweet, put his arm around me and said it was nice to meet me.

Someone took my photo with Ronnie. I have no idea who, but it was really sweet. I'm only 5'2", in heels I'm 5'6"- I towered over him.

He seemed totally down to Earth- no pun intended.

Now whenever I see videos of Lemmy & I, I notice the same thing happened a lot where folks I don't know took our pictures together! I'd love to have a photo of Dio & I together.

I also was at Heaven & Hell, when Dio sang for them (I was Lemmy's guest). I was just floored to be watching them play and hearing him sing!"
Nancy Elizabeth (San Francisco)

Dio

'Killing the Dragon' Tour
Chronicle Pavilion, Concord, CA
29th August 2003

Killing the Dragon
The Last in Line
Stargazer
Stand Up and Shout
Rock and Roll
The Mob Rules
Dream Evil
Rainbow in the Dark
Holy Diver
Heaven and Hell

"LOVED HIM! I remember riding around with my ex boyfriend at 15 years old in his 1969 Mach One Mustang (it was a vintage car, I am not that old. Giggles).
We were listening to 'Heaven and Hell' and 'Die Young' full blast!!! Great times and great memories. Ronnie James Dio was the best!"
Kimberly Cole Zemke (Jones, Alabama)

"As a young teenager in mid 1980's during my musical taste formation years I was totally under the influence of bands such as Motörhead, AC/DC and I liked punk music scene as well.
I was also discovering great bands that left huge mark in music history before my time such as Deep Purple, Led Zeppelin and Black Sabbath.
I was listening to Black Sabbath with Ozzy and then I came into touch with two albums that Black Sabbath made with Ronnie

James Dio 'Heaven And Hell' and 'Mob Rules'. I really liked those two albums and I still do.
Ronnie James Dio voice was always amazing!
Thru the years after that initial introduction to Ronnie James Dio I have followed and respected his great work and contributions he made to Heavy music scene.
He was one of the best vocals of all time and should be remembered as that!"
Darko Ivanovich (St Louis)

"Seen him with Sabbath back in '82 in Kansas City on the MOB RULES tour. A band from Canada named Rabbit opened for them."
Freck Wilkinson (Bowling Green, Kentucky)

"It used to drive my friends crazy that I wasn't a fan of Black Sabbath. Never understood the appeal. Now I get it, but back then it was lost on me.

Ozzy wasn't a great vocalist at all and their music was heavy but there was no melody. I understood that they were groundbreaking, but they bored me. I wanted something faster and a bit heavier. The thing was that if you were a metal fan the holy grail was Sabbath. They were the alter at which all metal heads kneeled and bowed in reverence and if you weren't a fan it was blasphemy. Then a friend of mine put a record on his turntable (back then the primary source of music was the vinyl record).

I had no idea what he was putting on and I hoped to Christ it wasn't Sabbath. I heard 'Iron Man' so much back then that I could hear that nasal whine in my sleep. When it started I shook my head and then the sludge cleared and those vocals! Those lyrics! Never, no never again! Listen to me and believe what I say if you can never, this is the end you know I've seen the faces of doom and I'm only a man. My mouth fell open and I sat there in silence until it ended. "Who is that?" I asked in astonishment.

This was exactly what I was looking for. It had the heaviness that I craved, and those lyrics! Much to my surprise it was Black Sabbath. 'Falling Off the Edge of the World' became one my favorite songs. It even trumps 'Heaven and Hell' but not by much. It was that moment that I became a fan of Sabbath. There was melody, and Ronnie's lyrics. The band never sounded this good and my God those songs!

'The Mob Rules', 'The Sign of the Southern Cross'. The thing was that as a band Sabbath had never moved beyond the doom style, but now they were experimenting more and it was all because of Ronnie. His voice allowed the band to travel into new directions and move away from the simplicity that they had been mired in. There was nothing that Ronnie couldn't do. Black Sabbath became a better band because of his input. It didn't last long of course but we still have the albums. Were they perfect? Of course not but they're snapshots of a time where Sabbath became better than they had been.

That was a memory that I will always look back on because without Ronnie I may not have explored beyond thrash metal and I would have never listened to Black Sabbath. I can tolerate 'Vol 4' and 'Master of Reality' but to me there's nothing better than 'Heaven and Hell', that is easily one of the greatest metal albums ever created. I still listen to that and I'm amazed at the differences between the two eras.

'Heaven and Hell' was a defining moment in metal that energized the genre. It proved that without Ozzy, Sabbath could go on, and

they did. Dio clearly saved the band and because of him the world of metal became a better place."
Michael Noe (Barberton, Ohio)

"All I can say of RJD is how much I loved his early work on Rainbow the best but he was a nice addition as Black Sabbath's lead singer when Ozzy left.
Dio's solo career was also impressive, with the whole HM genre starting to grow stale, he still had a razor's edge."
Richard A. Tucker (Miami, Florida)

" \m/ DIO \m/ "
Vinnechi Vrock Sins Pettachio (Philadelphia)

"I can just say he was a fantastic man from what his very good friend told me, they were really close!! And on stage it was touching to see him a few years before he died he sounded amazing!!"
Dana Joseff (New York)

"Ronnie James Dio had one of the greatest voices in rock history. I was first introduced to him on Black Sabbath's 'Dehumanizer'. What an introduction to such a powerful voice on such an amazing album. I went on to discover 'Heaven and Hell', 'The Mob Rules' and 'Live Evil', along with the DIO album 'Strange

Highways' and then the entire amazing DIO back catalog.
I have been a fan ever since, even picking up the 'Best of Rainbow' along the way but my true introduction to Ronnie's work with Rainbow came upon my brother Jeff's tragic passing in 2008.

He had the 3 Rainbow studio albums plus the live 'Rainbow On Stage'. Maybe I had heard a small portion of this material before but discovered the albums in their entirety, such incredible recordings.
I have followed Dio's musical journey since hearing 'Dehumanizer' back in 1992 through to the most recent Heaven And Hell releases. I recently even found a rare treasure of two of the Elf albums on one disc and heard some of his earliest work. I think I own almost every recording he has been a part of. I don't think anyone but Ronnie James Dio can say they were a part of so many amazing bands and recordings.
I was also lucky enough to see Dio live twice and Heaven And Hell once.
The first Dio concert experience was definitely unforgettable for two reasons. The incredible show and what happened afterwards. June 3rd 1998 at Pops Nightclub in Sauget IL. just across the river from St Louis ,MO. I was only twenty years old at the time and went to the show with my friends Brian and Jenel. Over the course of the evening pounding down Jägermeister and Bud Light every trip to the bar, enjoying the show until I got kicked out near the end. Standing outside by Brian's car waiting on my ride along came one of Sauget's finest brutal corrupt cops. Still remember that pricks name till this day.
He asked me what I was doing and abruptly grabbed me by the throat and slammed me up against the car. I naturally pushed away in self-defense. On the way to the station I was being told how him and his buddies at the station were going to kick the shit out of me. Fortunately that didn't happen.
I was awakened to my surprise upon posting bail that I had an assault on a police officer charge. He claimed that I punched him, a complete and total lie. Well a year or so later after many continuances the officer did not show, so all charges were dropped. He most likely was one of the corrupt Sauget police busted around that time for many different reasons of misconduct. Thought it would make for interesting reading so I included it here.
Back on track it was an amazing show seeing him at such a small venue for the first time. I missed out on the opportunity to meet Ronnie that night but my friend Brian made sure I ended up with

two autographed fliers from the show.

I went to see Deep Purple, The Scorpions and Dio at Riverport Amphitheater July 20th 2002 with my late brother Jeff. What an incredible concert experience that was. We had a little help having all the fun we had that night if you know what I mean. Another awesome performance from Ronnie James Dio! Oh, the Scorpions and Deep Purple were pretty awesome too.

The final time seeing Ronnie in concert was with Heaven And Hell, Alice Cooper and Queensrÿche. One of the best concerts I have ever seen. September 23rd 2007 at The Family Arena in St. Charles, MO.

The perfect smaller arena venue, for a show like this. It was supposed to be me, again my longtime friend Brian and my brother Jeff going to the show but upon my brothers tragic passing on August 7th of that very same year I got my friend Clay to go in his place. It was hard to even go but the amazing show that evening took my mind off of things for a night. Thank you Heaven and Hell, Alice Cooper and Queensrÿche!! Ronnie James Dio you will forever be missed in the music world.

Rest In Peace Ronnie. Maybe you and Jeff are rocking out up there!"

Jeremy Decker (St Louis, Missouri)

"I met Ronnie James Dio on the Sacred Heart tour in Philadelphia back stage! Although it was a very brief meeting for he was sure to personally meet each and every fan, he was the nicest and most gentlemanly man I had ever met. Taking time out of his busy schedule to chitchat with me about astral projection. It was so refreshing to talk to someone of his stature about something so mystical and spiritual that we along with countless others have experienced! Now I battle my own demons with the big C word! You will live on forever in our hearts, minds and souls. And I hope to continue our conversation when we meet again!
RIP"

Cynthia D'Ambrosio (Croydon, Pennsylvania)

"I first became familiar with RJD when he was in Black Sabbath. That's when I was just beginning to learn about Metal.
I thought he'd been their singer forever so to me that was Sabbath. When he left the band, that was a big deal and a major blow! What would his new band be like?
'Holy Diver' was one of the most influential albums of my High

School years just amazing! An addicting album you had to hear again and again all the way through! I reviewed it in my High school newspaper. I really wanted to spread the word about this amazing new band! I had yet to ever attend a concert but my chance finally came in January of '84 when Dio played the Santa Cruz Civic with special guests Black n' Blue (featuring future KISS guitarist Tommy Thayer) It was the end of that tour but the summer of that same year when 'Last In Line' was released the band started that tour at the Santa Cruz County Fairgrounds with Whitesnake and Ronnie Montrose's Monstars. Think about that Ronnie, Jimmy Bain, Cozy Powell and Ronnie Montrose are all no longer with us!

The first time I met Ronnie he was doing a signing at booth at the Foundations Forum Convention in 1991. He had just rejoined Black Sabbath and the "Dehumnizer" album was about to be released.

When I began working with our TV show Reality Check TV he became a recurring guest on our show.

A very funny moment was when I interviewed him for the album 'Killing the Dragon'. I told Ronnie our camera man named Dragon Dave was really disturbed about the title of the CD.

Ronnie not missing a beat said "Well we were going to call it 'Killing The Dave' so you saved yourself on that one Dave!"

It can't be empathized more he was hands down the absolute nicest guy in all of rock n' roll! At every after show when he was meeting the fans he wouldn't just sign autographs and move on. He gave every last person individual attention. He spent quality time with everyone back there. He would ask them how they liked the show and thank them for coming. He would ask each person after signing their stuff and taking photos if there was anything else they needed. He truly did love and care for his fans. I think any celebrity or rock star should follow this example when meeting their fans.

Ronnie would remember my name. Each time we'd meet he'd light up and say "Danny! How are you?" and give me a hug. To this day aside form Lemmy I've never met a famous person that was appreciative and gracious towards his fans. I thank you Ronnie for the great music, memories and pure kindness you showed.

Danny Shipman (Reality Check TV, San Francisco,Ca)

'Holy Diver' Tour
Civic Auditorium,
Santa Cruz, CA
6th January '84

Stand Up and Shout
Straight Through the Heart
Shame on the Night
Children of the Sea
Holy Diver
Heaven and Hell
Rainbow in the Dark
Man On the Silver Mountain/Starstruck

"I would like to share my experience with Dio and how I came across his music and the impact it has had on my life.
As a teenager in the eighties, due to a neurological condition known as Hydrocephalus, I spent a lot of time in and out of surgery which stymied my doctors quite a bit considering my ailment is normally contracted in the womb or as a result of head trauma, neither of which I encountered. I first showed symptoms of the condition at 14 years of age and was diagnosed with it at 15. I was relieved from the pressure in the brain with a shunt, which normally would require repair or revision perhaps once maybe twice in a lifetime, dependent on the occurrence of trauma to the head. I'm now 48 years of age and have had a total of 38 operations on my condition. Allow me to explain what occurred between the years 1982 through 1986.
Caught up in the pop music and subsequent music videos of that period, I felt that Michael Jackson, Madonna, Hall and Oates and the top 40, though occupying the charts and ears of my brother and his friends were lacking the emotional pain I felt having to deal with hydrocephalus for the rest of my days. My folks weren't

wealthy enough for cable and MTV and I viewed the music videos of the day of a syndicated VHF station that only broadcasted for ten hours a day. One day, while viewing the pop music videos that never seemed to pacify the hurt and anger prevalent in my being after already having been operated on six times, I viewed Ronnie James Dio's video for 'The Last in Line' and the rest is history.

Albeit, this wasn't my first encounter with Heavy Metal music. I was already an avid admirer of Quiet Riot, Ratt and Kiss. However, that song spoke volumes to me and I immediately purchased the album and then subsequently, as funds became available, possessed 'Holy Diver' and 'Dream Evil'. Later on, once I discovered that he fronted Black Sabbath, those CDS soon followed.

To conclude, I believe that the lyrics to his songs were so real to me in my agony and depression that believe it or not, they carried me through those years of despair. I recall walking home from my first year of community college with my Walkman plugged into my sense of hearing and having Ronnie at my side carrying me through the pain and suffering I will endure through my life.

Since that time, my life has turned around completely through marriage and finding Christ. But you know what? To this day, I'll never forget Dio and the void he filled in my life through those trying times. I still listen to his music and am grieved at his loss, especially after viewing the pictures of him in the hospital bed. It so paralleled my own existence."

Michael Mrozek (Schaumburg, Illinois)

"It was the fall of 1969 in Auburn, a small town located about 25 miles from Cortland, NY, where Ronnie James Dio was raised and came to prominence. I had just started high school, and had, at that point, seen a total of two bands perform live: the first at my eighth grade graduation dance, the second an outdoor show over the summer, both by local bands. The novelty of hearing a "real" group perform live before our very eyes, rather than seeing them lip synch on television had not worn off. My friends and I were quite excited about an upcoming dance at Mt. Carmel, the Catholic high school across town, as we had heard that one of the members of this group "The Elves" had actually made some records, which was true stardom in our youthful eyes. We couldn't wait.

The evening arrived, and we paid our $1.25 to get in. Entering the darkened gymnasium, we were met by a sound both exciting and slightly frightening: an unbelievably loud, but clean, hiss from the stage, which we recognized after a moment as idling amplifiers.... LOTs of them, with multiple pilot lights glowing in the dark. Budding musician wannabes that my friends and I were, we had all gone stag to check out the band, and huddled up to the stage to take in the gear before The Elves took the stage.

The biggest amps we had seen to date were small by even local standards. We were agog at what we saw. A veritable wall of amplifiers, more on that one stage than the entire inventory of any music store we had been in to date. Stage right, two full Marshall stacks, with a Y-cord going into both heads for one of the guitarists, whom we would learn was David "Rock" Feinstein, Ronnie's cousin, and later founder of The Rods. We recognized the bass rig, which Ronnie was to play through, as dual Sunn cabinets, on their sides and stacked on top of each other with the head atop. Our initial impression of the microphone stands was thought to be a joke: they were set so low that we thought it must be a pun on the band's name, and that obviously when the musicians came out they would raise them to their proper height. Not so, as we discovered when they came out that Ronnie himself was 5'2" and David topped out at an even 5'0".

The large fluorescent gym lights abruptly went off, causing a squeal of delight from the crowd that lasted only a second when suddenly there was an absolute explosion of sound and light from the stage. Explosion is an over-used term, but not that night. It was literal, and it was real. Nothing prepared our barely-adolescent minds for what unfolded. The band: Dave Feinstein - guitar, Doug Thaler –guitar and vocs, Mickey Lee Soule – piano and backing vocs, Gary Driscoll – drums, and Ronnie Dio (he hadn't started using the "James" yet) on bass and lead vocs, played louder than we thought volume actually went. It was *unbelievable, yet immediately apparent that it wasn't just the number of amplifiers used, but the power and command of the playing of the instruments that really gave this band its force.*

Ronnie could not honestly be called the "star" of this band. Not yet. They were truly a group of five equals, all extraordinarily proficient on their instruments, and in their songwriting, as the few tunes that they announced as "one of our own" showed. Ronnie did 3/4th of the lead vocals, Doug the others. Ronnie, however, quickly showed extraordinary depth and breadth in what he was capable of singing. The powerful growl and gravel in his voice that is so well known and loved by those of us who are fans of his later work was matched by a smooth, sheer beauty on the more tender numbers. We were stunned when the band came out for their second set and Ronnie said "Some people wanted to hear something from Abbey Road, so we're going to do the whole thing." The album hadn't been out that long. We were amazed that a band could learn that complex a piece so quickly, and how Ronnie was able to effortlessly nail the sweetness of Sun King or Something, and when Doug, Mickey and Ronnie joined together on "Because" it was truly one of the most beautiful things I had ever heard.

We were lucky to grow up where and when we did. I saw The Elves play at our high school dances about 10 times between that first show in the fall of 1969 and spring of 1973 when I graduated. The final time I saw the band was shortly after Doug Thaler left, an evening in which I got to meet Ronnie face to face for the first and only time.

There are many recordings of Ronnie's early years with Ronnie & The Red Caps, Ronnie Dio & The Prophets, The Electric Elves, and The Elves, which I have hunted down through the years. It was by hunting down and listening to his earliest recordings that I got an appreciation for the career development that had led to the performer I saw throughout my four years of high school. There is an extraordinary amount of officially unreleased material, live and studio, which stands as a great legacy to Ronnie the performer. Some of it, thankfully, saw the light of day a couple of years ago when the "And Before Elf...There Were Elves" CD was released. Imagine how thrilled I was to open up the sleeve and discover a photo that I had taken inside: Mickey Lee playing the piano, which was taken at the first performance in Auburn after the name change from The Elves to Elf, at St. Alphonsus School gym in Auburn, a show which I promoted as the 18 year old president of the church's high school youth group. I had accumulated by that point what I felt to be a whole lot of knowledge about Ronnie James Dio the musician, but that night I got to learn a lot about Ronnie the man.

By that point, the band had grown far past being a local sensation. The first LP "Elf" had been released, and the band was regularly playing national stages opening up for acts such as Badfinger, Edgar Winter, Cactus, Alice Cooper, Jo Jo Gunne and more. Three hour high school dances were well in their past, they now performed the standard sets that were the norm on national stages at the time: 45 minutes for the opening act, 60 minutes for the headliner. Taking advantage of some dead time between road trips, I somehow managed to convince Valex, their Ithaca-based booking agency, to sign a contract for a full three sets/three hour dance for less than the price they were commanding for a 45 minute show. Overjoyed at my "coup", I should have realized at my young age that when something sounds too good to be true, it usually is.

The night of the big event arrived. It was a relatively small church/school gymnasium, and I had hired three extra off-duty policemen as security for the parking lot, to sweep kids either into the gym and forking over their three-dollar admission, or leaving the premises and missing the show. Such was the band's popularity that the steady stream of paying customers finally abated half an hour before the end of the show. The road crew arrived and set up as usual, when about 10 minutes before the start of the show, the head of the crew told me there was "a problem" and I would need to meet with the group's leader: Ronnie.

The band had just arrived. Somehow, it had never been communicated to them that they were expected to go back to their days of three hours of music, and the head of the crew believed the band would blow their stack when they heard. He hadn't even said a word to Ronnie, just brought me up to the side of the stage and introduced me as "the kid in charge." He explained to Ronnie that this was not their usual 1 set show, and I nervously held the contract in my hand preparing to defend my position. I had no need. Ronnie just mildly smiled and said, "So we'll play three hours" as nonchalantly as could be. He turned to Mickey, said "give them some piano", and the band kicked off with "Sit Down Honey (Everything Will Be Alright) and never looked back. 43 years later, people still talk about that night, and several of the photos I snapped from the side of the stage circulate around the Internet.

By this point, although all four members were of equal proficiency, something had happened that made Ronnie truly emerge as the star of the band, and the reviews were beginning to say so. At the end of the show, I was awash with joy that we had raised a lot of money for the church, and in the process had given my hometown an incredible night of music. I had a couple of shots left on my cheap, instamatic camera, and asked Ronnie if he would pose for a picture. He said "sure, but let's get Mickey Lee in here too" and threw his arm around Mickey's neck and drew him in close for my photo. That's the Ronnie that I remember: gracious to an awestruck teenager, never afraid to give more than expected, and always willing to share the spotlight.

That particular picture, unfortunately, was in poor lighting and came out unusable. Maybe what I was supposed to remember wasn't the image, but the lesson. I never saw him perform live again, but I know many people who did, and have friends who were close to Ronnie until his last days. They all describe his kindness and graciousness, and I can certainly attest to that myself. He's known for many things: the voice, the devil horns, the mystical imagery, but for me, if I had to describe Ronnie James Dio based on my brief interactions with him, I could say only one thing: "What a gentleman!" Not a bad way to be remembered, is it?"

Mike Donohue (Syracuse, NY)

"He's with us (my BFF!) Count on it! He brought us closer together too!! I believe he is with us from beyond. Your experience with him was not by accident just as mine is not. I totally believe Ronnie is

greater than met the eyes here on earth. He's AMAZING and so darned Prophetic, Spiritual and Insightful. We ROCK!! \m/x\m/ "
Dawn Marie Burns (USA)

"Damn, I saw his last tour with Heaven and Hell with my son. He passed later that year. What a loss."
Robert Dunn (Brandon, Florida)

"I saw Dio many times. Even at the Fox in Atlanta. Holy Diver!"
Sam Satterfield (USA)

"Saw Ronnie many times in Dio, Sabbath & Heaven and Hell! Grandaughter listens to Dio already at 7 years old!
Never met Ronnie, to me he is metal greatest singer!"
Jeff G. Shiner (Whitehall, Pennsylvania)

"Lock Up The Wolves tour, at Brady Theater in Tulsa. I took the license plate off my car and brought it into the show- I wanted Ronnie to see it, it was an Oklahoma vanity plate that said DIORULZ. Not only did he see it, but he took it and held it up for the audience to see as well! He handed it back to me and my night was made. The plate still hangs in my garage today."
Troy Nelson (USA)

"Here's a little awesome memory from DIO. My husband went to see his idol in concert many many times. Remember back in the day when everyone would light their lighters during a certain song? Well my husband had a lighter that shot a flame bout 10 inches. DIO was on the stage singing and saw this huge flame comin from the lighter. DIO pointed to him, gave him a 'thumbs up' and said, "that's rock n roll!!!"
How cool to have your idol, speak to you outta a crowd of thousands!! Needless to say that is quite a memory."
Jennifer Tresher (USA)

"I seen Ronnie in Tulsa, Oklahoma in 1985 the 'Sacred Heart' tour. He was and will always be the best singer.
He is the man with the golden voice."
James McIntosh (Keifer, Oklahoma)

"I discovered Ronnie James Dio on the rock station while I was working at a jewelry shop in 2014 at age 24.
The station played 'Holy Diver' and 'Rainbow in the Dark'. Though I learned he was no longer with us, it didn't start occurring to me how much I had missed until I really began to explore his other songs and albums.
I watched his music videos, interviews and concert videos and almost felt a sense of mourning for what I had missed.
I would look back at some of my high school photos and say to myself,
"I should have been seeing Heaven and Hell live instead of wasting my time with that idiot ex boyfriend!!" Haha...
At some point, I came across a mesmerizing portrait of Ronnie by Dale May online. I knew I wanted to draw it someday, and finally in February 2016, I got myself a charcoal set, having never used the medium before, and made this, my first ever charcoal drawing.

Drawing Ronnie's face was like meeting him in person in a way. It's so awesome how someone can live on beyond death through their creations, in this case Ronnie's music, and continue to inspire others like me to create as well.
Now, even my 5 year old will tell you if you ask him what is your favorite music? "DIO!"
"Rock and Roll Eyes", 9x12 charcoal on watercolor paper."
facebook.com/artbyashleylacons
Ashley LaCons (Lacey, Washington)

"Dio was a kind man and really cared for mankind. Seen him in a very small venue in Dallas, Texas in '83 – 'Holy Diver' Tour, that's where it started, the love of Metal Music! Thank you for being so kind my man! You Rock!"
Grady Pilkington (Texas)

Ronnie's last show August 29th 2009

"My introduction to Ronnie's music came in 1980, when I was a freshman in High School, and my boyfriend bought the album 'Heaven and Hell'.
As soon as I heard the music and Ronnie's amazing voice, I was hooked!
I won't take your time with my entire musical trip down memory lane, except to say that I have NEVER missed a tour and was present at the filming of the videos recorded at the Spectrum in Philadelphia in August 1984, his recording of 'Evil or Divine' filmed at the Roseland Theater in 2002, and his live recording from Radio City Music Hall in 2007, where I had the pleasure of having my photo with Ronnie, my husband and myself included on the DVD. Hopefully this shows the dedicated fan I am, but it doesn't go nearly far enough.
As a kid, I was always trying to fit in. When I heard 'Heaven and Hell', I went back to all the music Ronnie had recorded previously, and found the charm of Elf as well as Rainbow.
Listening to Ronnie tell everyone to follow their rainbow, and not to 'talk to Strangers' spoke to my soul somehow. To me, the songs helped me to pursue my own dreams, and not to let others pull me off my path. They said if you have passion to pursue it.
I read every magazine article I could find, and saved them all. Yes, I still have many!
In my heart, Ronnie always held a special place and I defended him in every Ozzy vs. Ronnie argument successfully. I even got a die-hard Ozzy fan to admit that he secretly liked and respected his music, but since his brothers were massive Ozzy fans, he could never tell them. ☺
It was through Ronnie's website that I met my current husband, another massive Dio Fan.
We met in the chat room back in the days when you could actually still chat without having some jerk show up and say nasty things. It was there I made many friends including some I am still great friends with for life, like Genady, Max, Carol and Steve, who went on to become Ronnie's tour manager.
We were fans for life and loved not just the music, but the man behind the music for his wise nature and articulate passion for anything he talked about, be it sports, music or beer.
When I met him for the first time after a show at the Birch Hill, in Old Bridge NJ, I put out my hand to shake his. He looked at me and said, "That's not how we do it!" and he pulled me in for a massive hug. I was in shock and was instantly Star Struck (no, the song isn't about me thank God!) I cried the entire way home

because I was so happy that he was even more generous with his time than I could have imagined, taking his time with me and each and every other fan. He was amazing.

As the years progressed, I got to know Wendy from taking photos of the shows and sending them to her for use as she wanted. For every show we attended for years, she was gracious enough to put me down for a photo pass and 2 after-show passes. It was heaven, and I never took it for granted (because we didn't always get in!).

When we were fortunate enough to see him, he was always a gentleman, and as I got to know him personally over the years. When Wendy was traveling with him, I was also fortunate enough to meet and talk with her as well. What a wonderful woman.

My collection of after-show passes grew and from those meet & greets his sense of humor also became more apparent and I truly felt blessed.

I was fortunate enough to be at the last show Ronnie ever performed in Atlantic City, NJ. I somehow have to think that I was meant to be there that night, with my husband who also loved him dearly. I think we would have felt incomplete somehow if it wasn't that way.

We learned of his illness early on and I sent letters of inspiration. I was devastated to hear when we lost him and of course we made the trip to Los Angeles for his memorial. It was moving, fitting and perfect in every way. I am still devastated.

I know he would be proud to know how much he influenced my life, from helping me overcome awkwardness to spending my life with my best friend that I met through his website, he was always there for me.

I visit Cortland regularly and always bring flowers, and I talk to him every day from my car. I know he hears me, as he has already told me so.

Thank you to Ronnie, Wendy, Steve and so many others, for bringing me into the Dio Family, and always know he is close in all our hearts, no matter how much time passes.

We Rock!"

Pat Kibby (Dunellen, New Jersey)

Aftershow Jones Beach NYC 2007

**Aftershow Mohegan Sunday 9/9/2007.
Vinnie Appice, Steve Mignardi, Ronnie James Dio
and Pat Kibby**

*"It all went down in the sleepy little suburb of Schaumburg IL at a tiny club called The Jackhammer at 1450 E Algonquin Road, Schaumburg, IL on April 11th, 1997. I myself was born in Illinois and was living in River Grove at the time.
Now why such a small dive like that was chosen to record what Dio himself considered to be his 'first official live album' (he hated*

the Intermission release) seems questionable. But from what I know about R.J.D., he much preferred smaller and more intimate settings so that he could connect more with effectively with his audience and that night he sure did!

Between Ronnie's powerfully intense performance and the insane enduring energy of the crowd, it was collectively an explosive experience to behold!

My friend Bob and I were the first ones to arrive at around 6:30 PM and the doors opened at 7:00. So we had to stand around and wait a half hour in the snow and subarctic temperatures (this was still Illinois remember, and it was supposed to be Spring.) When Bob and I finally got in we found that this Jackhammer's place was a very small venue. It used to be a dance club called Toto's so there were some disco balls hanging from the ceiling, a few pool tables, about five food bars, with booths, seats, and barstools everywhere. There was a small dance floor in front of the stage that at least 500 people were already crammed onto. The place held a maximum capacity of about 1000 people, although I think that night there was way more than that!

We then had to wait about two hours listening to the DJ's music picks before the first opening band Raddaka came on. They were ok, but nothing to get your knickers in a twist about. But by the time they were through the audience was getting more than a little anxious, and that's when they gave the announcement that the second warm up band My Dying Bride was going on next. The crowd moaned and groaned and after about an hours worth of intermission they eventually shambled up on stage...and really blew! In my opinion there shouldn't be any opening bands unless they somewhat have the musical integrity of the headliner. We came to see Dio! Get to it already!! We were sweating our asses off in that tightly packed area by the stage and the perspiration was coming down in buckets!

After they finally finished (we had been there for roughly four hours now) people began shouting in a Troglodyte chant, "Dio...Dio...Dio!" Then seemingly in response, the stage curtain was pulled back to unveil Vinny Appice's drum kit and the drunk lunatic behind me started yelling, "DIO!!!! D...D...DIO!!!! DIO!!!!" And I was like,"Hey, relax dude, it's only the drums!" But then about 5 minutes later the moment I had been waiting for nearly 10 years finally happened... Dio strolled out, grabbed the mic, and fiercely and took the stage! The crowd suddenly sprang to life and the overall response was extraordinary! But I could barely see Ronnie through the tall heads of the people in front of me (and also because of his diminutive stature), but I skillfully managed to shimmy into a better position to see him more clearly. He was followed by Larry Dennison, Tracy Grijalva, and lastly Vinny Appice! I was happy to see that Vinny was looking healthy after his recent bout with pneumonia, and glad that I actually got to see him instead of just some fill in stick-man.

They opened the set with "Jesus, Mary, and The Holy Ghost", a song I was originally not too enamored with, but a dynamically amped up performance was given that night. The complete set list in addition to that song was as follows:

Straight Through The Heart
Don't Talk To Strangers
Holy Diver,
Vinny's drum solo
Heaven And Hell
Double Monday
Stand Up And Shout
Larry's bass solo/Hunter Of the Heart
Mistreated/Catch The Rainbow,
Tracy G's guitar solo
The Last In Line
Rainbow In The Dark
The Mob Rules

And the three encores:
Long Live Rock 'n' Roll
Man On The Silver Mountain and
We Rock!, the ultimate closing song in my humble opinion!

After "Straight Through The Heart" the crowd again began chanting "Dio...Dio...Dio...", and Ronnie mentioned in response that, "Somebody must have told you we're doing a live recording here tonight, huh?" This just confirmed the rumor I heard earlier and made it absolute truth, turning this into a truly historic evening! Soon after "Straight Through The Heart" concluded, Dio asked us all to step back a bit from the stage because the people in front were getting squished together like sardines. This of course was cut from the live release, but you can still hear the glitch where it was removed at 5:35 on the CD. That night Dio said this particular show was one of the wildest he'd seen in awhile. There was frantic bellowing throughout the show, people (like me) singing along word for word with every song, and plenty of body surfing! And I remember there was this one hot chick next to us that was sitting on someone's shoulders and everyone around her was trying to lift up her shirt since she had no bra on underneath. They managed to get it over her boobs once, but she was too drunk to care. She just continued to salute the stage with her beer bottle shouting, "DIO!!! DIO!!! WOOOOOOOO!!!" Man, this was turning out to be a great night!

As far as Larry and Vinny go, the bass was pumping and the drums were pounding all the way through the set list, and my ears were still gloriously numb days after the assault! The sight of Vinnie live was much more riveting in person than on any previous videos that I've witnessed. And his drum solo kicked all forms of major ass! I remember Dio jokingly making the comment right after Mr. Appice finished his drum solo, "What would you say if we did something unplugged right now?" (Because it was highly fashionable in those days to release live acoustic performances of electric songs). Some annoyed audience member shouted, "Bullshit!", to which Dio responded, "That's the same thing I would say, bullshit!" "Heaven And Hell" rocked next and Dio expressed his appreciation for Chicago and the audience saying, "We do something easy now, we just want you to sing along with us. You've done this before. I mean... hey, the first time we ever played this song with the Sabs was... in Chicago. And you did it right, so lets try it again. Just follow me, just gotta sing the words Heaven and Hell. Here we go..."

Everyone was playing and sounding great, although I thought that Tracy G's stage presence just wasn't quite there during most of the songs. But maybe that was due to the fan's response to him. Throughout the evening the audience were quite often booing and giving him the finger, especially during his guitar solo. It's good that none of that harassment actually made it to the live CD. In fact there's one point I clearly remember during the song "Double Monday" that you can hear Dio addressing a particularly excessive bird flipper in the front row on Tracy's behalf by gently saying, "Fuck you..." and extending the finger to him as well. You can hear this at 1:53 on the disc.

Tracy Grijalva was also heavily criticized for not playing in the style of Dio's original guitarist Vivian Campbell. I don't even remember Vivian's successor Craig Goldy taking that much heat. I do know a lot of the older fans did not take well to the current darker direction Dio was heading, and the audience was not afraid to let it be known. But what they have to remember is that Ronnie James Dio himself was always in full control and captain at the helm of his own musical ship. Tracy was not influencing him that heavily that he could not disagree if it wasn't truly the direction he intended to go in. Many fans failed to realize that. I was not particularly fond of many of the newer 90's songs myself, but I personally felt that Tracy G added his own unique and distinctive guitar sound to the older classic Dio songs and breathed new life into them.

Larry Dennison's bass leading into "Hunter Of The Heart" was absolutely fantastic and inspired. It's a shame it was cut out from the live release, but I still have it on a bootleg that I bought at a convention about a month later in 1997. The official release did not brand itself onto CD until February 24, 1998.

During the encores (at which point I believe we were totally exhausting the band with our enthusiasm) the crowd got absolutely whacked! I could barely keep the records I had with me to get autographed safe from being annihilated in the mosh pit! But I somehow managed to push myself to the front of the stage and Dio smiled at me when I waved to him before the song "Last In Line" began, and then pointed at me after I took his picture. One of the most offbeat moments I captured on film that evening was right after the final song "We Rock" where R.J.D. was kind of casually cavorting with the crowd. Someone decided to hand him a beer as if to say, "Great job Ronnie! Here ya go man, you deserve this!" Classic stuff ;)

Then after the uproarious concert was over, and the smoked cleared and the dust settled, my voice was totally incapacitated from screaming on all eight cylinders. And my heart was pounding so fast I almost passed out due to it being hot as hell in there! But the concert as a whole was extremely awesome, and absolutely fabulous!!! To my delight the audience cleared out of the building rather quickly and I told my friend, "We are NOT leaving until we get some autographs!" Now Bob wasn't a huge fan like I was, but he was familiar with most of the popular Rainbow and Sabbath tunes. He even had a vinyl copy of 'Holy Diver' which he hadn't opened yet. And I stressed to him, "When you get home the first thing you should do is play it!"

Well this is where the story starts getting really good. I talked to group of stage hangs and staff members afterwards to find out the best way possible to meet Dio without backstage passes. They all told me the best thing to do was wait by the tour bus. So that's what we did and waited over an hour in the freezing cold. Just chilling and chatting with two other couples we met, who were also anxious to meet Ronnie James Dio. But it seemed like it was taking forever and one couple finally threw in the towel and departed, while wishing the rest of us good luck. "Quitters!", we smirkily shouted at them. They smiled at us and drove away, probably thinking we were bonkers to wait for so long.

The other couple that remained was this fine looking chick named Jean with this dude named Brian (who was only her friend, thankfully). She too happened to be an enormous fan, not unlike myself, and had the determination to try to sneak into a side entrance of the Jackhammer to save some time in finding Dio. Well, being no dummy I followed her saying we'd be right back and leaving my friend Bob and Brian behind in the cold. They thought we were wasting our time anyways. Jean and I walked through what seemed to be the kitchen on the lower level. We then seen some Spanish dudes in there who couldn't speak a lick of English waving to us to get out, so we acted like we did and turned around. But just as soon as they had walked back into the kitchen we continued on. Both of us made it through a maze-like corridor into another building adjacent to the Jackhammer. "Where the hell are we?", I said. But then as we both turned the corner Jean stopped cold, her eyes widened, and she pointed to an open door with a long haired seated figure inside with about 20 people around him. "Oh... my... god", she said. "THERE HE IS!!"

And yes, there in the small modest room casually chatting with the keepers of the backstage passes was the 'Man On The Silver Mountain' himself- Mr. Ronnie James Dio. The security caught us after she screamed bloody murder, and both of us were then forced to leave. We walked right past him into another hallway while she couldn't stop screaming, "RONNIE, WE LOVE YOU!!!" I grabbed her arm firmly saying, "If you don't stop screaming we're never gonna get him to sign autographs". She said something like, "I know, but I was so excited..." Then one of the security guys from inside the room came out and said, "If you want to get stuff signed afterwards that's cool, but you just have to wait until all the others are finished." I excitedly told him, "No problem man!", and we took off down the hall. That guy was ultra awesome!! Jean and I both were still trying to accept the fact that we were just standing in the presence our idol, close enough to touch him. I commented that it was like finding a hidden Easter egg! We both then decided that we should go back and get our friends, although we didn't really want to...

But alas, we returned to collect the ones of whom we rudely left in the dust and dragged 'em back with us through a different entrance. We navigated through the great labyrinth of hallways and once more made it back to the room of the great 'Neon

Knight'. And after waiting for about 15 minutes, a flood of people were evacuated and we all thought, "Great! We can finally see him..." We all entered the small room and didn't see anybody but security and a few other people at first, but then finally Dio appeared and none of us seemed to notice.. He was so non chalant that he seemed like one of us just hanging out. I was the first to exclaim, "Hey, there he is!" Ronnie was dressed in a black leather jacket with a black and white checkered scarf (and he must have been more than just a little disenchanted with our weather here...)

Now this is the part I can't believe... how nice this guy really is. He seems so unapproachable on stage, but in person he is really benevolent! I was falling all over myself to get ahold of the records I had with me so he could sign them! And after I composed myself I boldly stepped up to him, handed him the 45, and said, "Here's something I bet you haven't seen in awhile..." And what I actually handed him was the first ever original vinyl release by Ronnie And The Redcaps "Lover"/"Conquest" from 1958. You should have seen the look of surprise on his face when he saw it. "Where did you get this?" he asked incredulously. "It wasn't easy..." I said. Now remember in those days (the 1990's) finding internet information about the musical history Dio fought so hard to keep a secret was not as easily accessible as it is today. I had to do some major digging to find both the information on his past and how to get that record. It actually took a lot of legwork and I started that journey all the way back in 1991. My search led to The Counts Castle and this guy Bob Ellis who specialized in hard to find collectable records. He had connections to a music store in upstate New York where he found a copy of the 45 for me. Wasn't cheap either. And it turns out in 1958 something like only 1,000 copies had been pressed at the time of it's release...

He signed the "Conquest" side of the tiny red record and I was overjoyed! Then I asked him if he played trumpet on it. "Yes, and bass too", he reminded me. I thought, "Oh yeah, how could I forget!" "Now hold on to that one", Dio said. And since my friend Bob didn't bring his Holy Diver album (which he was now kicking himself for), I sold him a group photo of the band I had purchased so he would have something for R.J.D. to sign. Jean had Ronnie autograph her CD, while Jean's friend Brian had him sign Rainbow's Long Live Rock 'n' Roll album. Then I quickly got my camera and asked this woman in the room to take a pic of us altogether. (I didn't know it at the time, but I later found out that this was actually Wendy Dio his wife). Jeez, I'm still shaking my head at that dude Brian though. I mean, who wears a KISS shirt to a Dio concert, man?? (sigh...)

At this point I was still in a daze of excitement when my friend said,

"Why don't you have him sign the other album too?" The other album being referenced was in fact the first original issue 1972 ELF record. "Well I don't know if he would do that for me too…" I said, trying to sound nice and non encroaching. Dio then replied in a friendly tone, "If you want something, all you have to do is ask." Wow, this guy was the living embodiment of congeniality! The last thing I can remember saying to him that night was, "I know you're Italian, so am I. Do you also speak it?" To which he turned to me with a grin on his face and said, "Only the bad words…"

Unfortunately that's the last thing I was able to ask, although there were about a zillion other things on my mind. "Maybe next time", I thought as he was ushered out the door to an inconspicuous van that was waiting in the back alley. A member of his team said that he had to move quickly in the weather because they didn't want him getting sick. Then after reality finally began to materialize once again, I offered to send a picture to Jean of all of us and Dio after it was developed (yep, no cell phones with cameras either back then), and also one to Bob. She gave me her address to send it to, and also her phone number. Man, what a night! It was a real trip, thats for sure…

1.) Finally seeing my all time favorite singer in concert
2.) Being present for a live recording that Dio later considered the first 'live recording he was totally happy with' (unlike the 'Intermission' album)
3.) Getting to personally meet and talk to Ronnie
4.) Having extremely rare records signed
5.) Sharing the whole incredible experience with an attractive woman I met that night, and getting her phone number as well.

This was without a doubt the most memorable concert I've ever been to and one that hasn't, and probably won't ever be, equalled ever again.

On the way back to the car Bob and I eagerly discussed the nights events. He couldn't believe how nice of a guy Dio really was. "I told you", I replied. Then I said, "You'll definitely have to open that Holy Diver album now, right?" "Yep", he smiled.

I saw Dio two other times afterwards. The first was at Rolling Stones music store on 7300 West Irving Park Road in Norridge IL, on November 29th, 1999. I took a pic but my camera wasn't working too well that night, so the result was a pretty cool looking psychedelic triple negative shot. (The Rolling Stones sign in the background was me taking more photos after I left to try to fix the problem.)

The third and final time I saw Ronnie James was on October 4th, 2007 after I moved to Arizona, when he was fronting Heaven And Hell in Tucson. Alice Cooper opened for them. Didn't get to speak to him personally that night, but Dio sure gave one HELL (pun intended) of a performance!!

In addition to being an avid R.J.D. fan, I'm also an artist! I drew this illustration in 1997, around the time of the Jackhammer concert.

In 2002 there was a lot of talk about a possible Elf reunion concert with Roger Glover on bass, Mickey Lee Soule on keyboards, Ronnie on vocals (of course), David Feinstein on guitar, and possibly Simon Wright on drums. Although this reunion never came to pass, at that time I thought it really might actually happen. So I did a computer graphic image of the band as actual elves and titled it Return To Nevermore. It was based on the song "Nevermore" from the first Elf album, which sound was the most reminiscent of where Ronnie's music would soon be heading in the future. I seriously considered submitting this to the Fan Club for them to show it to Ronnie and somehow get his approval to use the image. Of course it never happened, although the picture did get some heavy circulation on the internet at that time due to my sending it both to Tapio Keihanen's Ronnie James Dio Pages and Padavona.com- Ronnie Dio's Early Years. And because of that, much to my surprise, it ended up on numerous R.J.D. websites and even landed in some fan made Dio music videos on Youtube."

Sal DiFatta (Spring Hill, Florida)

Sal DiFatta (Spring Hill, Florida)

"Favourite album of all time - 'Holy Diver'"
Boomer Simpson (USA)

"Awesome tour ('Holy Diver')"
Raef Decanditis (Iva, South Carolina)

"Had the pleasure of seeing Dio before he passed in 2003 at Sacramento CA as part of a 3 band lineup with Motorhead and Iron Maiden."
Stephen Grace (La Conner, Washington)

"Rest in peace Dio..."
Klocke Shelbi (USA)

"Simply the 2nd best front man in rock history and the best I ever saw. No one I saw could "control" a crowd like him. I wonder how many "Christians" were cheering to go to hell during his shows? (ps #1 is Mercury)"
Don Manuszewski Jr. (Ellicott City, Maryland)

"I live in Champion ohio we love DIO I have all his DVD and watch one of them every weekend the last show I seen live was Heaven and Hell I Cleveland in '09."
Robert Markle (Champion, Ohio)

"I love Dio more than anything. He was the 'Man on the Silver Mountain'.
God bless you Mr. Dio!"
Sam Satterfield (USA)

"I'll never get over Ronnie's death. He meant so much to me.
Not only was (and is) he my all time favorite singer, he was (and is) one of my all time favorite songwriters. And he was a class act who carried himself with class and dignity and always showed the thoughtful, intelligent side of Heavy Metal.
Whenever I listen to Ronnie I feel both happy and sad at the same time. I really miss being able to see him live and hear new music from him. Like I said, I'll never get over his death."
Erik Rupp (Menifee, California)

"One of my Goal's was to see my Fav Singer. Never did.
He was from Cortland,N.Y. & I from Syracuse,N.Y. About an Hr. Drive South. Cortland even has a St. Named after the King of Rock 'n' Roll. This makes feel close to Him.
I have His Greatest Hit's CD & Play Whenever I'm in the Car.
Thank you. <3 & Peace."
Shelly Davis-Hill (Syracuse, New York)

"God bless him."
Megan Coppock (USA)

"I miss this Entertainer (MAN). How special was he for all of us."
Frank Nestor (El Paso, Texas)

"Thank you for givin' us the best music of all of time!!!"
Lorraine Cunningham (Bay City, Michigan)

"RIP Ronnie. Never forget the time I had him slap my hand at the Beacon Theater in Manhattan, NY. He smiled and gave me a 'thumbs-up' while singing my favorite song ever, 'Heaven and Hell'. That was the 'Dehumanizer Tour'. Miss that man tremendously."
Guy Cusimano (Shirley, New York)

"Loved his music !!
R.I.P. Ronnie."
Angela Robbins (Berlin, New Hampshire)

"My how time flies!!"
Kathleen Bradley (Fresno, California)

"His vocals still give me strength and inspiration through the hard times and shitty days...and makes the good times even better. Rock on dark Angel. \m/ "All together, you'll never be stronger than me"!!!! \m/
Only time I saw him was on the 'Sacred Heart' tour...rocked my world forever!!!"
John Robert Mondoux (Las Vegas)

"His music will live on forever!!!!"
Michael Ryan (Colorado Springs, Colorado)

"A TITAN indeed!! Giant is just to small of a word, for a Man that has so much Talent & Inspired & influenced so Much of the known World with his Voice & Music.. 'The Mob Rules'..
Rest in peace" ICON".. RJD...!"
Joe Madera Guzman (Los Angeles)

"R.I.P. Ronnie James Dio. You are missed every day.
I sometimes hear you singing in the wind."
Mellisa Minor (Fort Wayne, Indiana)

"My Mom passed two days before Ronnie, same year. Cancer too, sigh..."
Rob Taylor (Wilsonville, Oregon)

R.I.P Ronnie James Dio.
Am so thankful I had a chance to meet you when you was in CANTON OHIO at the Hilton Hotel.
Had a great time hearing you sing with my daughter .

We spent a good 2hrs with you that night. Best night I ever had.. You are truly MISSED."
Theresa Haren (Louisa, Virginia)

"I would comment but I 'Don't Talk To Strangers'
:P lol RIP RJD"
Jay Walden (Idaho Falls, Idaho)

"We miss you Ronnie you have touched so many people with your singing you will always be the man with the golden voice."
James McIntosh (Kiefer, Oklahoma)

"No one like Ronnie James Dio. Sadly missed. Jamming with Lemmy I believe."
Tim Cline (Grand Marsh, Wisconsin)

"RIP Ronnie! ✌❤☺"
Lefred Melancon (Galliano, Louisiana)

"Rest in peace."
Julian GC (Brooklyn, New York)

"RIP Ronnie we all miss your great voice."
Dave Van Asch (Coon Rapids, Minnesota)

"I only have 1 story & that's when I saw Dio perform at Roseland Ballroom in New York City & the night he performed he gave a clinic & I've been a long time fan of his & I still have the ticket stub. But I'm digressing. My memory of him was when I turned from the stage & when I turned my gaze back toward the stage he was looking right me smiling flashing the peace sign. That truly was a forever moment for me & I said many times that it was that moment that I became a Dio Disciple for life.
He really cared for the fans because he was one of us & one with us. I still miss him to this day among all the legions of fans & still wish he was with us now."
Philip R Booker (Seattle, Washington)

"I went to high school with Ronnie. He was a great person.
I saw the beginning of his talent. He performed locally and also at school. Wherever he was the place was packed full. He also had a wonderful family. He his mother would accept our visits to their home. It was wonderful to watch him grow as a talented

entertainer. While in high his group Ronnie and
I went to high school with Ronnie. He was a wonderful person. He would perform locally and at the high school. Where ever was the place was packed full. It was wonderful to watch him grow as a gifted singer. He came from a wonderful family. His mother always accepted us friends welcomed us to their home. Ronnie will live on in my heart."
Kristen Rinaldi (USA)

"Hard to believe it's been six years."
Ted Green (USA)

"RIP Dio the great."
Thomas Culotta (Camden, Delaware)

"San Bernadino, California Was The Place Where I First Saw This Incredibly Small Man Walking Out Of A Man Made Cave On Stage In 1983, His Voice, His Lyrics, His Love For His Fans Made Him The Strongest & Tallest Man I've Ever Witnessed Performing Live In My Life. Thank You Mr. Dio"
Tom Fritschi (High Point, North Carolina)

"Wow living in east Alabama going to a small town school, yeah we, my friends, we were taking a lasting lashing for not listening to the mainstream, but DIO was mainstream in our world."
Lee Moore Sr (Las Vegas)

"My first concert was Dio 'Holy Diver' in San Antonio Texas."
Frank Cisneros (Crystal City, Texas)

"Remember in 1992, he was on the third song, and fan pulled him off stage when he was singing War Pigs. Ronnie Jumped back up and pointed at the guy. He continued on and the drunken fan remained. Great concert, but no concert I seen was ever and will ever be forgotten by DIO or the road beers and party's.
Time to remember \m/ "
Bob Karlick (USA)

"His were some of the best shows I've ever seen!"
Cory Czarapata (Greenfield, Wisconsin)

"Rest in Peace!!!"
Ar Lene (San Antonio, Texas)

"I miss him more and more every day, that voice!!"
Angie Holt (Jefferson City, Missouri)

"I wish I could share a memory of seeing Ronnie James Dio live in concert or have the pleasure to say that I met the father of heavy metal himself but I can't for you see I was born too late and in a generation who has no idea who he is.
I am the first generation in my entire family to even recognize his name and it saddens me deeply to not be able to share his music with someone who has such an infatuation for Ronnie's kickass vocals as I do.
All through middle school, high school and now in college, I listened to nothing but Dio, anything from Elf to Heaven and Hell, if he was singing I was listening because his music continues to be so therapeutic for me.
As many, I suffered most of my life with immense anxiety and depression which would lead to self harm and the only voice I recall hearing though all though those tough times was Ronnie's. Always there though thick and thin, I owe my life to his music and will make sure his music lives on through my children.
Long live Ronnie James Dio, a true artist."
Beverly Villagomez (LA)

"Ronnie's voice still gives me strength and inspiration through the hard times and shitty days. I had the extreme pleasure of meeting Vinny Appice a few years back (such a cool cat, and so down to earth). I told him that people look up to Batman and Robin as their superheroes where my superheroes were Ronnie and Vinny. He sincerely thanked me for that comment.
Ronnie was the true Dark Knight.
Thank you for honoring his memory...sincerely.
John R. Mondoux (Las Vegas, Nevada)

Here's a Dio memory Ian. I was 15 years old. Holy Diver I think was the concert it was Dokken and Dio. My friend Jason had a 67 Mustang. I took a check out of my poor hard working mother's checkbook and went to the convenient store and cashed it. It was that easy back then. Anyway my friend Jason and I missed most of Dokken but we seen all of Dio.
It was awesome and well worth the ass whoopin' I received when my mother found the carbon receipt. Long live Dio!!!!"
Brian Sockwell (Kansas City, Missouri)

"Such a gem of a human being Dio was. He's far from perfect, for sure, but his flaws just give him more character. (Though I wish he and His Ozzness had gotten along, a deficiency which I hold against both of them equally.)"
Jeff Healey (Utah, USA)

"At the Paramount Theater in Seattle in '83 with the local brand new sensation Queensryche opening the show.

I was the backstage guest of my relatively new voice teacher Maestro David Kyle, who taught Geoff Tate how to sing as well as Anne Wilson, Layne Staley and many many more superstars, anyway, I digress.

Dio signed this and was very gracious to me and spent quite awhile talking with the maestro while I stood dumbstruck. I consider Dio, as well as Tate, to be two of my largest influences. I studied with the maestro until his passing in 2003.

I have been on the music scene in Seattle, well since then. The cassette you can see in the picture is one of my first bands.. I'm currently singing in two original bands here in Seattle. One Gun Shy as well as BlackLine... I cannot quit, I tried once and was miserable. So I sing for the love of it and I thank R.J.D. for opening such a tremendous gift.

I would like to finish this with a quote from Maestro David Kyle - Vocal music is an attempt to take the whole human being and projected into space. You take a part of you that is most private most personal most Inward and you hurl it out into space. You projected as far as you can. That gesture of opening this whole region of the body results in an enormous spiritual release and it is felt by other people with tremendous impact."
Billy Young (Washington)

'Holy Diver' Tour
Paramount Theater, Seattle, CA
1st October 1983

Stand Up and Shout
Straight Through the Heart
Shame On the Night
Children of the Sea
Holy Diver
Stargazer
Heaven and Hell

"I Saw Ronnie James at a small club in the early 90's, the Birchhill in old Bridge New Jersey ...I met him a couple times over the years, at the Birchhill was one of those times!
The first time I saw Ronnie was with Rainbow when Scorpions opened up for them in like 1981 on the 'Blackout' album tour... But The First time I Saw Dio Was At L'Amour In Brooklyn, Ny in '83 on 'Holy Diver' tour.
Then I saw him with Metal Maria from Megaforce Records backstage at the Spectrum in Philadelphia like 1984 'Last in Line' tour...got to hang backstage with him and all.
By far the sweetest guy you'd ever want to talk to, so polite and so interested in what you're talking about total respect.
Then of course we caught him on his last couple tours in 2007 & 2008 with Priest ...doing Heaven and Hell, stuff which was killer.
We had VIP passes and tickets for 2007 literally up against Tony Iommi. That last tour we saw him in 2007 before he got sick was phenomenal what a killer bill - Heaven and Hell, Motörhead & Testament at The Pnc!"
Zipper~Head (USA)

Dio

'The Last in Line' Tour
The Spectrum, Philadelphia, PA
25th August 1984

Stand Up and Shout
One Night in the City
Don't Talk to Strangers
Mystery
Egypt (The Chains Are On)
Holy Diver
Heaven and Hell
The Last in Line
Rainbow in the Dark
Man on the Silver Mountain
Long Live Rock 'n' Roll
The Mob Rules
We Rock

"I'm good friends with Keith Gruber, Craig's brother bass player for Elf, Rainbow, Gary Moore, way back in Homer on Cortland St. Craig had his gig stuff taking up half the downstairs and he was always playing bass.

When Elf played at Sugget Park for free in 1972, my first concert with Keith, they had a tractor trailer with a door that opened up on the side, that was high tech! The band was crowded in but the show was one of the best with lights and all.

They played a free show in 1974 same thing, great show they also had a bus and the story goes he stopped the bus to get someone walking a ride.

To me Rainbow was the band that Ron put together with old Elf members. I saw Black Sabbath with Ozzy in 1979 before the breakup. I've seen Craig with Gary Moore on you tube, still friends with Keith his dad had a limo to transport around Ron and Craig are still a great influence to players everywhere Craig had a special bass in his name."

Scott Brown (USA)

"A short story about a place called 'The Spot' in Allegany, NY. The Elves played there frequently. One time the marquis read:
'Live: Elves!' - People thought it said 'Live: Elvis!'
Needless to say, the line was pretty long waiting for Ronnie and the band."
Dane Clark (USA)

"Ronnie James Dio is one bad mutha fucka!!!!
I've seen him in Dallas, Tx. and for such a little dude, he can sing his ass off!!! Some male singers kinda sound a little gay when they scream and hit the high notes, but not R.J.D. He sang with balls !!
He also was such an awesome lyricist, he will be greatly missed. I'm sure he is still rocking his ass off in heaven, cause I can't imagine heaven without rock 'n' roll.
I know we will see you jam again one day Ronnie, so sail on, sing a song, carry on.... We rock!!!!!!"
Adelita Mendez (Arlington, Texas)

"I recently talked to Ronnie's roommate in college, he said Ron was the cleanest clear cut guy not a hair out of place. The years went by and they met up again and Ron had long hair and a beard and he said 'what happened to you' and Ron said 'I joined a rock and roll band'!"
Scott Brown (Homer, New York)

"In 1994 I believe it was, I was to go see DIO at an old movie theater called The Huntridge in Las Vegas. For some reason I can't remember they rescheduled. The night they rescheduled for, we were having an outrageous rainstorm and if you know Vegas, that don't happen often. You could barely cross the streets without being washed away, we were flooding BAD. Coincidently, my pool league team was also shooting in 1st place the same night.
I blew EVERYTHING off and pretty much swam my way up to The Huntridge. NO WAY WAS I MISSING SEEING MY ROCK GOD RONNIE JAMES DIO!!!!
He put on the most amazing show and I got the honor of shaking his hand and just being up so close to him was worth everything to me! I miss him but celebrate his birthday every year on July 10th, which also happens to be my daughter's birthday!!!! How cool is that?!!!
R.I.P. RONNIE - You'll never stop rocking my world!!!!"
Teresa Lee Henry (Las Vegas, Nevada)

Dio

'Strange Highways' Tour
The Huntridge Theater,
Las Vegas, NV
19th July 1994

Jesus, Mary & the Holy Ghost
Strange Highways
Don't Talk to Strangers
Pain
The Mob Rules
Holy Diver
Heaven and Hell
Man on the Silver Mountain
Evilution
Give Her the Gun
Stand Up and Shout
The Last in Line
Rainbow in the Dark
We Rock
Here's to You

"I never met Ronnie but I feel as though he's told me a ton of stories and life lessons that have shaped me into the person I am today.
His lyrics painted pictures into your mind of anything your mind was capable of imagining. That was what Ronnie was really about. Making you think about life and what surrounded it, making you feel like you could achieve the impossible, go to magical places you could only be taken to through Ronnie's words and to stand up and shout for what you believe in!

Never is someone more empowered through life than when they listen to Ronnie James Dio's music. The fierceness of Black Sabbath, the organic rock 'n' roll of his years with Elf, the early power metal vibes in Rainbow. Ronnie was as versatile as a singer gets.
When Ronnie sang of pain and heartache you felt it in your gut. More times than not, Ronnie would get you pumped up for the next thing life would throw in your face. The guy had a heart of gold. He was a true gentleman to his fans and his music will forever stand the test of time."
Bailey LaPatka (Mankato, Minnesota)

"I was 15 when I first heard Black Sabbath's 'Heaven and Hell'. Ronnie James DIO changed my life.
His voice and talent stunned me for the better from then on I was able and fortunate to attend His funeral services in California and visit often to His resting place.
I will forever miss Him on this plane of existence and plan to see Him one day in this beautiful Universe I share with Him.
Thank you RONNIE JAMES DIO for your contributions to the Music World, love always."
Lisa E Fury (Chicago, Illinois)

"My first introduction was in 1982. I bought the 'Mob Rules' album. I saw it, liked the cover, so I took a chance. That was the beginning of a 34-year run as a fan of Ronnie's.
One of my favorite memories was seeing him on the 'Master of the Moon tour'. That is one concert I will always have good memories of, cause my brother and I went together."
Mike Sorenson (Chicago, Illinois)

"I met DIO in Phoenix Arizona on the 'Last in Line' tour...
The charisma of this man & his mannerism will always be the thing I remember the most. I remember asking him what he thought of the tour up to that date his response – "it's a magical time."
Long live the King RJD."
Mike Palma (USA)

"I had seen Dio twice before this in Jersey; once with Rainbow & once with Sabbath. Both shows were awesome!
Then in I believe '94, he was playing the Beacon Theatre in NYC solo.
I happened to know the manager at the time & showed up with a

friend. He let us in and we were right at the stage. It was awesome seeing him so close and putting on an awesome show!
I even spoke to him briefly after the show! What a kind, funny man! It was wonderful seeing him in a small theatre and meeting him! I will never forget that show!
Wish I had more to tell but he was taken from us way to soon! RIP Ronnie & thank you for years of great music!"
Sue Punke (Clayton, DE, USA)

'Strange Highways' Tour
Beacon Theatre,
New York, NY
9th June 1994

Jesus Mary & The Holy Ghost
Strange Highways
Don't Talk to Strangers
Stand Up and Shout
Pain
The Mob Rules
Holy Diver
Man on the Silver Mountain
Heaven and Hell
Evilution
Hollywood Black
The Last in Line
Rainbow in the Dark
We Rock
Here's to You

"I have seen Ronnie on many occasions, but on this one occasion I had the honor of meeting him my first time.
It was for the 'Angry Machines' tour and Ronnie was playing at a bar on 8th street in Colorado Springs Colorado.

Ronnie came out on stage and was putting on an amazing show. I had a picture of Ronnie and took my chance and reached out to give it to him. Ronnie took the picture and I motioned for him to sign it. He took it to the back and gave it to someone. To be honest I never thought I would see it again.

Well the show ended and people started leaving the bar. I was busy drinking a few and was getting ready to leave when suddenly a guy comes up and tells me that Ronnie wanted to see me.

I was allowed to take my 2 cousins back with me as well. I remember walking to his bus and thinking about all the stuff that I had thought that I would tell him if I ever got the chance to meet him and here he was! The Man on the Silver Mountain right in front of me and I was tongue-tied.

When Ronnie was on stage he was the biggest Giant I had ever seen and here in front of me was a gentle, humble intelligent man. I told him 'I always thought about what I would say to you if I ever had the honor of meeting you and now I don't know what to say except that you are like a fork or a spoon in my house'. He interrupted me and asked, where I was going with this story and laughed. I told him he didn't understand but I was comparing him to these items in my house because they get used everyday, just like he did. I told him my mom, brother's, sisters and everyone who comes into my house knows you, you get used everyday. He had a puzzled look on his face, gave me a hug and shouted 'behold my greatest fan', while my big mouth cousin was hollering, 'no Ronnie, I'm your greatest fan'.

We hung out for a while after this and he told me that had to be the best and most unexpected compliment he had ever had. He gave me an autographed CD, autographed my picture and put me on a VIP list in Denver for the night after. He told me before we parted ways.

'Thank you ! Thank you for letting me BE Ronnie James Dio!'"

Josh Cordova (Trinidad, Colorado)

"Many years ago, there was a club called The Avalon here in Chicago. Wednesday nights were generally rock/metal night, and after our own band rehearsal, I'd go there to hang out for a while.

My friend Rob and I had been Dio fans since Rainbow, and seen many Dio concerts and played 'Heaven and Hell'/ 'Mob Rules' music countless times.

He was a metal icon to us.

So one night, Rob and I are hanging out watching a local band in the jam room. I walk out of that room and proceeded down a short hallway to the guy's bathroom. While I'm walking in one direction, coming towards me are Ronnie and the guitar player from Enuff 'Z Nuff Derek Friego. I stopped as they walked past me to make sure I was seeing this for real and not something else due to my alcohol and other intake for the evening.

I wasn't hallucinating; it was really Ronnie James Dio. He was in town for a gig. This was during the record that he had done with Rowan. I quickly found Rob and said "Come with me right now!!!!". Ronnie had walked back to the less noisy hallway where I just saw him and Rob and I stood right next to him.

Rob had also consumed the same type of intake as I, probably more, because he looked at me with his very red glassy eyes half open and was confused as to why I pulled him out of the jam room. "The guy standing right next to you is Ronnie James Dio" I said closely to his ear so he could clearly hear me.

He looked to his left and all of a sudden, his glassy red eyes got real big with a look of surprise and amazement. He put both arms around Ronnie and said, "I love you man!!" and gave him the kind of hug that lifts Ronnie off of the floor until his legs are dangling in the air.

I was laughing pretty hard as I was asking Rob to put him down which he did. It seemed to catch Ronnie off guard, but he was cool about it. I went to look for a pen or something to get his autograph. A local waitress gave me a pen but was very clear that I needed to give it back to her. I gave it to Ronnie and asked for his autograph, which he did. But then...he held onto the pen. Damn...what now?

I stand patiently to the side, as others by now know it's him and he's signing for everyone. Now, I should have just let it go because it's a stupid pen, but she did do me a favor and I told her I would give it back to her. I guess there was a pen shortage in the club? So, with the slightly clouded mindset, that I had going I politely say to him "Ronnie, the waitress wants her pen back". I guess that he wasn't real happy about that and I didn't hear his reply clearly due to the music, but he did say something along the lines of "something...something...Fuck her!!!" Then he turned around and ignored me from that point on. That's just great...way to go genius I think to myself.

So, as I walked away feeling bad that I may have momentarily angered one of the best singers in the business, plus a waitress, I did continue to laugh about the visual of Ronnie's legs dangling in the air from a big hug that my friend Rob gave him.

I still have the autograph that reads "To Neven,,,Magic...Ronnie James Dio"

I miss you Ronnie."
Neven Trivic (Chicago, Illinois)

"Ronnie James Dio. A man, a legend.
He made such an impact on so many people as well as the music industry. Even if you are not a fan or know his name, you know at least one song. Whether it be from his solo music or with Rainbow, Sabbath or Elf.
He will always be missed, but I know that he is in a better place! His spirit will definitely live on! My kiddos will know who he is, for sure. We love you, Dio!"
Destiny Ann Cagle (Dexter, MO)

"I once had a chance to meet Dio and actually I was able to chat with him about a lot of things. But most of our conversation was about music. I told Dio about the impact that his music had on my life.
When Dio asked me which song of his was my favorite, I told him "Stargazer". DIO looked at me, smiled and said "Mine too." Thanks Ronnie, for talking to me, and all the great music. I still miss you."
Erick J. Dobson (USA)

"I saw Ronnie James Dio, in 1982, Lexington, Kentucky, 'Holy Diver'. One of the best shows I've ever seen.
Christopher Lane (Indianapolis, Indiana)

"Hearing Dio's 'Rainbow In The Dark' in the summer of 1983 would change my life as a disco fan forever. I became a metalhead overnight, loving ALL that was metal...But Dio was MY band. Gathering any and all Dio and Dio related memorabilia, I was the quintessential Dio fan and anyone within the tri state area knew it.
Little did I know that on August 2, 1990 during a 'Lock Up The Wolves' pre tour show in New Haven that had only 300 invitees that a friendship of 20 years would be spawned. It was at this show that Ronnie & Wendy would befriend this then 500lb Dio fan. I would see the band 5 more times on this tour...All on Ronnie's dime and all with Ronnie's heart, soul and time given to me.

In 1992 during Black Sabbath's 'Dehumanizer' tour in NYC at what would be my 1st of 10 shows on that tour, I didn't think Ronnie would even remember me. Sure, at 500lbs I didn't look like the average person. Still, in my mind a man of Ronnie's stature could never remember me. I couldn't be more wrong. During the sound check in NYC, Ronnie stopped the band to come outside to make sure I was all set for the gig.

From 1990 to 2009 I have many variations of the above situations...As do many other friends and fans of Ronnie's. I honestly can go on forever. My band opened for Dio in '97, I had coffee with Ronnie's mom, dad & him in his childhood home, I'm in 2 of his DVDs, had many heart to heart conversations with him, I took the front cover photo for 'Dio's Inferno: Last In Live' CD, lost massive amount of weight thru his friendship and love for me...It goes on & on.

I was fortunate to spend the entire week on the road with Heaven and Hell on what would be Ronnie's final tour. At Ronnie's finale in Atlantic City I thanked him for everything, wished him a safe trip home, told him I'd call him in a week and we hugged goodbye. As we walked away in different directions he turned and said, "Big Jim, wait up!" He ran to me and gave me the biggest hug he'd ever given me be fore saying goodbye a second time. I believe he knew. He knew something. Maybe not everything...But something.

When the diagnosis became public I made a decision to not call him. I knew full well he'd console me by telling me he'll beat this and will be okay. I did what I thought was the next best thing. As a working musician I bought a 'Get Well' before every gig, had every one attendance sign it and mail it to him. I wanted him to know he was loved from afar. I'm sure he knew

It's been said you shouldn't meet your heroes. They typically don't turn out to be who you think they are. In Ronnie's case...Who ever could have thought he would be the kind hearted soul he was? Long Live RJD!

Oh...Any Dio band mate, fan or crew-member who knows me knows me as "Big Jim"

Jim Hoefelt (Seymour, Connecticut)

"I met Ronnie on October 1st 1980 in Chicago. I had gotten back stage because I knew one of the bouncers working the concert. This was the "Heaven and Hell" album tour dubbed as the "Black and Blue Tour".

I caught the eye of one of the roadies for Sabbath and gave him a little note to give to Ronnie.

It said "I know who Muriel is and she says hi"...I guess he was intrigued at the reference to Muriel and "Starstruck". He told the roadie to take me to meet him and I got to shake his hand and get my little diary autographed with my red pen...he wrote "To Rita, Magick from Ronnie James Dio".

I will never forget that day and I was only 17 and to my mind, the note was a silly game I was playing, never expecting to be invited to the dressing room.

The late 70s and early 80s in Chicago were awesome days for concerts and I went to as many as I could with a couple of my friends.

I even got my son into Dio's music and he now is the proud owner of a Dio Limited Edition ASG guitar. (#49)).

Rita Caywood (Federal Way, WA)

"In junior and/or high school, I went to a boarding school, wherein, as a weird teenager, I was introduced to American Rock n' Roll. In particular, I worshiped Ronnie James Dio and had a 'shrine' dedicated to him.
As evidence, my private 'DIO shrine' was as depicted in the attached photograph wherein it shows cut-outs and posters from various magazines, such as Metal Edge, Hit Parader and Circus amongst others. This so-called DIO "shrine" was on a wall facing right in front of my desk where I did most of my studying. It was my inspiration and helped me concentrate on my academic pursuance and achievements.
As nostalgic and silly as it seemed to be, the music of DIO still helps me to remain strong and overcomes various adversaries and hardships to this very day. In short, DIO helps me survive.
Regrettably, I didn't go to any of his concert before he died, but I visited "Dio Way" in Dio's hometown of Cortland, New York, as can be seen in another photograph."
Ronald Mok (New Jersey)

PLEASE CAN I ASK YOU ALL TO TAKE A LITTLE TIME OUT TO LEAVE A REVIEW ON AMAZON FOR THIS BOOK.

It was a great deal of love and effort contacting all of you from all around the world about your memories of the late **Ronnie James Dio**
I just wish that I had been able to receive even more replies as you all deserve to be in there.

If you have enjoyed this book, why not check out my similar book on Lemmy as well?

Many thanks to each and every one of you that has either contributed or purchased this book, I love you all.

OOOOO

Other Books Available By Ian Carroll

Music Books

The Reading Festival: Music, Mud and Mayhem – available in full version or as 1970's, 1980's and 1990's separate editions.

From Donington to Download – available in full version or as 'Monsters of Rock' and 'Download Festival' separate editions.

Lemmy: Memories of a Rock 'N' Roll Legend – The fans, the artists, the whole 'shebang'. Number 1 on Amazon in the UK, USA, Germany, France and Canada.

Welcome to Cornwall Coliseum – covering the iconic South West UK venue that played host to shows by all the big stars of the 70's & 80's – Black Sabbath, Iron Maiden, Rainbow, Paul McCartney, Whitesnake, Saxon, The Clash, KISS, Eric Clapton and hundreds more

King 810 – an introduction to the band

Horror Books

The Lovers Guide To Internet Dating – The dangers and the stalkers

Demon Pirates Vs Vikings – Scandinavian horror

Valentines Day – Gypsy curses

My Name Is Ishmael – Demons are everywhere...

A-Z of Bloody Horror 'A' is for 'Antique Shop'

A-Z of Bloody Horror 'M' is for 'Warning: Water May Contain Mermaids'

A-Z of Bloody Horror 'P' is for 'Pensioner'

All available on Amazon, on Kindle and in Paperback for bargain prices